A-level
Success

Economics

AQA

Practice Test Papers

James Beere
and Keiran
Matthews

Edited by
Denry Machin

ACKNOWLEDGEMENTS

The author and publisher are grateful to the copyright holders for permission to use quoted materials and images.

Cover & P1: © zhang kan / Shutterstock.com
Paper 1, Extract A data: © 2011 TMA
Paper 1, Extract B: © ASH
Paper 1, Extract D: © Crown copyright 2016, reproduced under the Open Government Licence
Paper 2, Extract A: © ONS / Crown copyright, reproduced under the Open Government Licence
Paper 2, Extract D: © Crown copyright 2016, reproduced under the Open Government Licence
Paper 2, Extract E: © 2016 MGN Limited
Paper 2, Extract F: © 2016 Independent.co.uk
Paper 3, Extract A: © Parliamentary Copyright, reproduced under the Open Parliament Licence
Paper 3, Extract C: © Parliamentary Copyright, reproduced under the Open Parliament Licence
Paper 3, Extract D: © Sterling Exchange Rate Index – © Bank of England, Bankstats database

Every effort has been made to trace copyright holders and obtain their permission for the use of copyright material. The author and publisher will gladly receive information enabling them to rectify any error or omission in subsequent editions. All facts are correct at time of going to press.

Published by Letts Educational
An imprint of HarperCollinsPublishers
1 London Bridge Street
London SE1 9GF

ISBN: 9780008179045

First published 2017

10 9 8 7 6 5 4 3 2 1

© HarperCollinsPublishers Limited 2017

British Library Cataloguing in Publication Data.
A CIP record of this book is available from the British Library.

Series Concept and Development: Emily Linnett and Katherine Wilkinson
Authors: James Beere and Keiran Matthews
Editor: Denry Machin
Commissioning and Series Editor: Katherine Wilkinson
Project Editor: Rachel Allegro
Peer Reviewer: Rob McGrath
Proofreader: Louise Robb
Cover Design: Paul Oates
Inside Concept Design: Ian Wrigley
Text Design and Layout: Aptara®, inc.
Production: Lyndsey Rogers and Paul Harding
Printed in Great Britain by Martins the Printers

MIX
Paper from responsible sources
FSC C007454

FSC™ is a non-profit international organisation established to promote the responsible management of the world's forests. Products carrying the FSC label are independently certified to assure consumers that they come from forests that are managed to meet the social, economic and ecological needs of present and future generations, and other controlled sources.

Find out more about HarperCollins and the environment at
www.harpercollins.co.uk/green

Contents

Introduction: How do I use this book?

This book contains exam papers (papers 1, 2 and 3), mark schemes and model answers written in the style and format of the assessment required for the AQA A-Level Economics specification examined from May/June 2017 onwards.

While this book will help you to develop your understanding of the content of the course, its main focus is to help you develop the **skills and exam techniques** you will need to maximise your grade in each of the three exam papers. As such, this book is the ideal companion to a traditional textbook or revision guide.

We recommend that you systematically work through the question papers, mark schemes and example student responses contained in this book as part of your revision schedule. As well as providing you with valuable practice of exam-style questions, the questions and exercises will help you to understand how examiners award marks and what you need to do in order to achieve a top grade.

We suggest you follow the procedure below in working through this book:

 Attempt a question

Attempt an exam question from one of the papers, e.g. a data response or essay question.

We suggest you try to do the question in as close to exam conditions as possible. You don't need to unplug from your music, but should find a quiet space where you won't be disturbed. Make sure you have everything you need with you: pens, highlighter, pencil, ruler, paper and something to use as a timer. If you really must use your phone as a timer, turn it to the 'Do Not Disturb' mode; Snapchat and Instagram will still be there when you are finished… we promise the world won't end!

When you are ready, the first step, of course, is to read the question carefully. You are also advised to highlight the **command word** (see p. 10). The next step is to plan your response. A few key pointers in the margin, a quick mind map, a flow diagram or an outline structure are all useful ways to do this planning.

Once you have a good grasp of the question and the structure of your answer, start writing. Write your response out in full. Try to avoid writing in note form as you want to make the practice as real as possible. You don't need to stick strictly to question timings but we do suggest that, as you become more confident, you time yourself and work towards the following:

 In the exam you have, on average, 1.5 minutes per mark. For example, a 9-mark question should take you about 13.5 minutes to complete (9 marks × 1.5 minutes).

 Remember, as well as writing your answer out in full within this time, you must also have read the question carefully, read the relevant context material provided and planned the structure of your response.

When writing out your essay response your focus should be on producing the best answer possible in the time available. You are likely to be very tempted to answer the questions in this book 'in rough' or, worse still, 'in your head'. As challenging as it is, our advice is to try to complete as many questions as you can in full. That's how you get the best marks possible in the real exam. Practice makes perfect, but only if it is perfect practice!

 ## Self-assess your answers

The next step is to self-assess your answers. You do this by rating your responses against the set of grade descriptors provided. Consider each descriptor carefully and rate yourself on a scale of 1 to 5 for a 25-mark question or 1 to 3 for a 9, 10 or 15-mark question.

If you think your response fulfils a particular descriptor, give yourself a higher rating. If you think your answer does not fulfil the descriptor or only partially fulfils it, award yourself a lower rating and identify it as an area for improvement.

 ## Analyse the example responses

After you have attempted a question and self-assessed it, read the example response provided in the mark scheme. Each question has a top level example response that demonstrates the knowledge and skills needed to do well.

As you read the example response, carefully consider how you could improve the quality of your written answer, particularly in terms of the grade descriptors you identified as areas for improvement.

Look at how the example response fulfils each of the grade descriptors you used to self-assess your answer. For the longer response questions, each example answer is annotated with comment boxes to aid you in your analysis. For example:

> Demand is the quantity of a good or service that consumers are willing and able to buy at different prices over a period of time. A fall in the demand for cigarettes is shown by a shift to the left of the demand curve from D1 to D2 in fig. 1, resulting in a fall in price from P1 to P2 and a fall in the quantity traded from Q1 to Q2.

AO1: Shows sound knowledge of the meaning of the term 'demand' and the effect of a fall in the demand for cigarettes.

 ## Self-reflect

Finally, reflect on your response by writing down at least one thing you did well (WWW – *What Went Well*) and one thing you could have done to improve your response (EBI – *Even Better If*).

 ## Have another go

Did we say finally? We meant finally for that one question. This book is full of questions, so attempt another question and repeat the process. Focus on developing your skills in one or two of the areas you identified for improvement in your self-assessment. As you become more confident, also work on completing questions under timed conditions (i.e. roughly 1.5 minutes per mark).

Structure of the exams

The AQA A-Level Economics course specification is divided into two main sections – microeconomic issues and macroeconomic issues.

You will be assessed through your performance in **THREE** exam papers:

Paper 1 Markets and market failure	Time allowed	Total marks for paper	Weighting
Assesses mainly your knowledge of *MICROECONOMIC ISSUES.* **Section A:** Data response questions with a choice of one from two contexts Total marks for this section = **40 marks** **Section B:** Essay questions with a choice of one from three questions Total marks for this section = **40 marks**	2 hours	80	33.3%

Paper 2 National and international economy	Time allowed	Total marks for paper	Weighting
Assesses mainly your knowledge of *MACROECONOMIC ISSUES.* **Section A:** Data response questions with a choice of one from two contexts Total marks for this section = **40 marks** **Section B:** Essay questions with a choice of one from three questions Total marks for this section = **40 marks**	2 hours	80	33.3%

Paper 3 Economic principles and issues	Time allowed	Total marks for paper	Weighting
Assesses your knowledge of *both* MICROECONOMIC *and* MACROECONOMIC ISSUES. **Section A:** 30 multiple choice questions Total marks for this section = **30 marks** **Section B:** Written answers linked to case study material Total marks for this section = **50 marks**	2 hours	80	33.3%

How do I choose the right questions?

As you will have noticed, both papers 1 and 2 offer you a choice of questions to answer – you must choose one from two contexts in Section A and one from three essay questions in Section B. Selecting the question that is best for you is an important part of doing well in the exam overall.

Only you know which are your strongest topics and, therefore, which might be the 'best' questions for you to answer. However, here are some things to consider when making your choice:

Choosing the best context

- **Be Selective:** In the interests of speed, don't try to read every context in full before deciding which one to answer. This will use up too much valuable time. Instead, read only the headings of the extracts, giving you an idea of the main themes. Then read the questions, identifying the main economic concepts and principles each question is focusing on.

- **Be Decisive:** Once you've made your choice, stick with it. You will lose time if you have second thoughts and switch between contexts – a problem that can be avoided by making the right choice the first time round!

- **Be Balanced:** You are unlikely to find the perfect context and the perfect set of questions. You need to pick the 'best fit' for your skills and knowledge.

Choosing the best essay question

- **Be Prepared:** Revise all parts of the course content thoroughly. Being selective about the topics you revise in preparation for your exams is risky and highly likely to backfire!

- **Be Flexible:** Don't walk into an exam fixated on answering a question on a particular topic. Consider all the options available to you before making your decision.

- **Be Thorough:** Make sure you read both parts of each essay question (the 15-mark part and the 25-mark part) and choose the one that will enable you to achieve the highest marks across both. It's no good writing the perfect answer to the 15-mark question only to realise that you know very little about what's being asked in the 25-mark question!

Assessment objectives explained

The assessment of your written essays will be based on your ability to achieve the following assessment objectives (AO).

Assessment objective	Description	Overall weighting (approximate)
AO1: Knowledge	Demonstrate knowledge of terms/concepts and theories/models to show an understanding of the behaviour of economic agents and how they are affected by and respond to economic issues.	29–31%
AO2: Application	Apply knowledge and understanding to various economic contexts to show how economic agents are affected by and respond to economic issues.	31–33%
AO3: Analysis	Analyse issues within economics, showing an understanding of their impact on economic agents.	21–23%
AO4: Evaluation	Evaluate economic arguments and use qualitative and quantitative evidence to support informed judgements relating to economic issues.	15–17%

How do I get the marks?

As shorter answer questions (2 and 4-mark questions) and multiple-choice questions (1 mark each) assess mainly **knowledge** (AO1), they tend to have a clear outcome, e.g. calculate the percentage change in price.

While accurate knowledge (AO1) is also important when answering longer essay questions (9, 10, 15 and 25-mark questions), your responses to these types of questions are assessed mainly in terms of your ability to **apply** (AO2), **analyse** (AO3) and **evaluate** (AO4). Because each of these skills doesn't have a single outcome, they are marked using something called levels of response.

Levels of response explained

When assessing your written response to an exam question, the examiner will refer to a set of descriptors before awarding it a mark. While the descriptors will vary slightly depending on the type of question being answered, there are a number of common areas (outlined in the table below) in which you must perform well to be awarded a top level response.

Assessment objective	Descriptor
Organisation	The overall structure of your response should be clear and logically sequenced, using paragraphs. You should also make sure you address all parts of the question.
Knowledge	You must show that you have a sound understanding of the main economic idea(s) presented in the question. To do this, you should do your best to use economic terminology appropriately and accurately. The economic theory, concepts and principles that you include in your answer should also be accurate and relevant to the question. Diagrams should be precisely drawn and clearly labelled.
Application	You must show that you are able to apply your knowledge of economics to the context of the question. To do this, you should use data from the contexts provided to support the main points in your essay.
Analysis	You must show that you are able to link your ideas using logical chains of reasoning. To do this, you should use connective phrases such as, 'this leads to...', 'as a result of this...' and 'this is because...' to clearly explain the sequence of effects resulting from an economic action or decision.
Evaluation	You must demonstrate that you are able to evaluate the range of possible outcomes resulting from an economic action or decision. To do this, you should use phrases like 'However, this depends on...' to consider the various alternative outcomes of an economic action or decision throughout your written essay. You must also make sure you provide a well-balanced response by considering both sides of the question, giving your opinion and backing it up with clear, well-reasoned justification.

The extent to which you are able to fulfil each of these descriptors in response to an exam question will determine the level of response you are awarded. The higher the level response you are able to achieve, the higher your mark will be. For longer answer questions, there are five possible levels of response – 5 being the highest and 1 being the lowest. In order to be awarded a level 5 response, your answer must fulfil all of the above descriptors. If some descriptors are only partially fulfilled, you will be awarded a lower level of response and hence a lower mark.

In addition to helping to develop your **knowledge** of the course content, systematically working through this book will help you to improve your skills of **application**, **analysis** and **evaluation**, as well as the **organisation** of your written essays so that you are able to fulfil the above criteria to the best of your ability. See pages 11–13 for more guidance on how to apply, analyse and evaluate.

Command words explained

Before answering a question, it is important that you take notice of the **command word** that is being used. Command words often, but not always, come at the beginning of the question. A command word is the word in the question that instructs you on the approach you should take when writing your response.

For example:

> With the help of a diagram, explain the effect falling real wages may have on households in the UK and what the government can do to improve living standards. **[9 marks]**

The command word in this question is **explain** (though it doesn't come at the beginning of a sentence). This means that you should give clear reasons for your response, linking related issues and ideas using logical chains of reasoning. You shouldn't just state points – you need to say how, in what ways, for who and why those points are significant to the question.

Examples of command words include:

Command word	Meaning	Assessment objectives	Questions types
Calculate	Work out the value of something.	AO1	Typically 2-mark questions
Explain, analyse	Give clear reasons, linking related issues and ideas in logical chains of reasoning.	AO1, AO2 and AO3	Typically 4, 9, 10, or 15-mark questions
Discuss, assess	Weigh up both sides of a statement before making a supported judgement.	AO1, AO2, AO3 and AO4	Typically 25-mark questions
Evaluate	Consider the range of factors, and the significance of each, affecting an outcome (*'However, this depends on…'; 'of these factors, the most significant is…'*) before making a supported judgement.		
Justify	Consider both sides of a statement, develop logical chains of reasoning and give your opinion, supporting your reasoning with clear evidence drawn from case material and economic theory ('…on the one hand… on the other hand'; '…<argument>… in contrast… <counter-argument>'		

Note that command words such as **discuss, assess, evaluate** and **justify** each assess the full range of assessment objectives.

How do I apply, analyse and evaluate?

How to apply

The skill of application is your ability to apply your knowledge of economic theory to the context given to you in an exam question. In order to do this well, you must first read the information provided to you in the exam paper so that you have a good understanding of the context in which you are writing.

You can demonstrate effective application in your written response by:

- making points related to the broader context of the extracts

- using specific examples and/or numerical data from the extracts

- making calculations from the numerical data provided

- including your own knowledge of relevant real world data, issues or events

Example of application:

These extracts have been taken from a student response written in the context of the cigarette market in the UK.

Student response – extract A
'As the tax per pack rose from £1.20 in 1990 to £6.25 in 2014, consumption dropped from 5.13 billion to 1.99 billion packs per year. However, there may have been other factors which contributed to this fall in consumption such as a trend towards healthier lifestyle choices...'

Application of numerical data from the extracts.

Application within the broader context of the cigarette market.

Student response – extract B
'The UK government could also attempt to modify the behaviour of consumers using nudge theory. Examples of this are the Behavioural Insights Team's (BIT) use of financial incentives and commitment devices such as pledges to reduce smoking...'

Application of the student's own knowledge (BIT not mentioned in the extracts but is relevant to the question).

How to analyse

The skill of analysis is your ability to link related economic concepts and ideas into *logical chains of reasoning*. In order to do this well in your written responses you must use connectives (see below) while always ensuring that your chains of reasoning are expressed clearly and are relevant to the question.

Some connectives linking cause and effect include:

this may lead to	as a result	this may result in
as a consequence	therefore	because
however	thereby	hence
in order to	the effect of this is	due to

Example of analysis:

Student response – extract C
'The demand for cigarettes may fall *due to* a fall in the price of substitutes, such as e-cigarettes. A fall in the price of e-cigarettes *may result in* more smokers substituting e-cigarettes for traditional cigarettes, *thereby leading to* a fall in the demand for traditional cigarettes.'

A logical chain of reasoning linking a fall in the price of e-cigarettes with a fall in the demand for traditional cigarettes.

How to evaluate

When responding to longer essay questions, the answer is almost always 'it depends'. Being able to weigh up a range of different factors and make a judgement on which are the most important in a given context is known as evaluation. Evaluation should occur throughout your written response, not only at the end of your essay in the conclusion.

In order to demonstrate effective evaluation in your writing, you must consider the full range of factors, perspectives and arguments that may impact an economic outcome. Common phrases that can help you to do this in your writing include:

However,	However, this depends upon	However, from the perspective of
On the other hand,	although	despite this
even though	in contrast	an opposing view is

Example of evaluation:

Student response – extract D
'The effectiveness of a tax in reducing cigarette consumption also *depends upon* the price elasticity of demand (PED) for the product. Demand for cigarettes is likely to be price inelastic as they are addictive and there are few close substitutes available. An increase in the price of cigarettes is therefore likely to lead to a proportionately smaller decrease in the quantity of cigarettes consumed, thereby limiting the effectiveness of an indirect tax in reducing cigarette consumption.'

This comment evaluates the impact of PED on the effectiveness of an indirect tax on cigarette consumption. It is followed by a logical chain of reasoning explaining the evaluative comment in the context of the cigarette market.

How do I organise my response?

One of the criteria you need to fulfil in order to achieve a top level response is to produce a **well organised** answer.

The best way to organise your writing will depend on the type of essay question you are responding to. However, there are certain things you can do in all of your extended written responses to ensure your ideas are well organised.

- **Speed plan** – Under the time pressure of exam conditions, you do not have time to prepare a detailed plan before writing your response to a question. However, it is important that you take a few minutes to 'speed plan' by jotting down a few relevant points on the question paper and arranging these in some kind of logical sequence. The main objective is to have the overall structure of the essay clear in your mind before you start writing out your response.

- **Write with the reader in mind** – As you write your response to an exam question, think about the person (your teacher or the examiner) who will be reading it. Ask yourself, 'Will the reader understand what I'm trying to say?' Go back and re-read the paragraphs you have written and, if necessary, make small changes to ensure your ideas are communicated as clearly as possible.

- **Use paragraphs** – Organise your ideas using paragraphs. Each paragraph should have a main idea that is clearly communicated in the opening sentence (the topic sentence). The remainder of the paragraph should develop the main idea using logical chains of reasoning and, wherever possible, accurate diagrams, evidence and examples from the information provided. It is also a good idea to leave a blank line in between paragraphs to clearly separate one paragraph (or main idea) from another.

- **Start with the economic theory** – It is good practice to outline the economic theory relevant to a question at the outset of your written response. This may simply be the definition of the key economic term in the question or may consist of a more detailed outline of an economic model that will form the basis of your written analysis.

- **Use diagrams** – Provided they are relevant to the question, diagrams can greatly enhance the organisation and clarity of your written work. However, it is important that your diagrams are fully labelled and that you explicitly refer to them in the body of your response using symbols.

- **Refer back to the question** – Make sure that you re-read the question repeatedly while writing your response, preferably before starting each new paragraph. This only takes a few seconds, but helps to ensure that what you write is on topic and directly relevant to the question. Also, try to deliberately link back to the question at least once in every paragraph. Use terms or phrases from the question to signal to the examiner that you are doing this.

How do I self-assess my own essays?

In order to develop your skills of application, analysis and evaluation as well as the organisation of your writing, you must take time to self-reflect on your responses. As a guide, we recommend you spend at least as much time marking and reflecting on your responses as it takes you to write them – you learn by doing <u>and</u> reviewing.

As a reminder, you should follow the five-step process outlined below to get the most out of this book.

Five-step process to self-assessment

Step 1: Rate your response

Read your response and rate it using the descriptors provided (see pp. 16–19). For each descriptor, give yourself a rating based on how well you think you have fulfilled the requirement. Ratings will range from 1-5 for a 25-mark question and 1-3 for a 9, 10 or 15-mark question. The higher the rating, the more successfully you will have fulfilled the descriptor. Try not to be too self-critical during this process but also try to be realistic!

Step 2: Award yourself a mark

Award yourself an overall mark by looking at the ratings you have given yourself. For example, if you are self-marking a 15-mark essay and you have rated yourself mostly 3s, award yourself a mark between 11 and 15 (a level 3 response as per the mark scheme on p. 17). The more 3s you have, the higher your overall mark within this band. If, on the other hand, you rated yourself mostly 2s, award yourself an overall mark of between 6 and 10 (a level 2 response).

Step 3: Read the example response for content

Read the example response provided. On your first reading, focus on the content contained in the response. Use the content of the example response along with the points under 'other areas for discussion' to develop your understanding of key concepts in the question. Use this to check that the content of your essay is accurate. Note that there may be points you have raised in your essay response that are not mentioned in the mark scheme but would still gain you marks.

Step 4: Read the example response for skills

Read the example response a second time. On this reading, focus on the skills of application, analysis and, if required by the question, evaluation. Look carefully at how each of these skills has been demonstrated. Use the comment boxes provided to help you. The comment boxes highlight some, but not all, of the skills being used.

Step 5: Reflect on your performance

Review the ratings you gave yourself when you self-assessed your essay and revise your overall mark up or down, if necessary. Identify at least one area in which you did well (**WWW** – *What Went Well*) and at least one area in which you could have done better (**EBI** – *Even Better If*).

After you have completed the five step process for one question, have a go at another essay question. Try to repeat WWWs and improve in at least one of the EBIs you identified in your next attempt.

Self-assessment frameworks

As you work through this book use the frameworks below to self-assess your performance.

> **Grade descriptors – 9-mark data response question**

Read your response and rate yourself on a scale of 1 to 3 for each of the descriptors below. Rate yourself 3 if you feel you have fulfilled the descriptor to a 'good' standard, 2 if to a 'reasonable' standard and 1 if to a 'limited' standard.

Assessment objectives (AO)	Descriptors	Self-ratings		
	In my written response, I have:	1	2	3
Organisation	used paragraphs to organise ideas clearly and logically			
Knowledge (AO1)	used economic terminology appropriately with few, if any, errors AND shown a sound knowledge of relevant economic concepts and principles with few, if any, errors			
Application (AO2)	effectively applied my knowledge of economics to the given context AND made good use of data to support my key points			
Analysis (AO3)	focused on developing a few key points that are relevant to the question AND developed my key points using clear, logical chains of reasoning			
Diagram	included at least one clear, accurately labelled diagram AND referred to the diagram(s) in the body of my response using symbols (e.g. P1, Q1)			

In addition to these areas, it is also important that you:

- respond to all parts of the set question

- use punctuation and grammar accurately

- complete your response within the time allowed (approximately 13.5 minutes)

Award yourself a mark out of 9

Level of response	Self-assessment	Max 9 marks
3	If you gave yourself mostly 3s	7–9 marks
2	If you gave yourself mostly 2s	4–6 marks
1	If you gave yourself mostly 1s	1–3 marks

Grade descriptors – 15-mark essay question

Read your response and rate yourself on a scale of 1 to 3 for each of the descriptors below. Rate yourself 3 if you feel you have fulfilled the descriptor to a 'good' standard, 2 if to a 'reasonable' standard and 1 if to a 'limited' standard.

Assessment objectives (AO)	Descriptors	Self-ratings		
	In my written response, I have:	1	2	3
Organisation	used paragraphs to organise my ideas clearly and logically			
Knowledge (AO1)	used economic terminology appropriately with few, if any, errors AND shown a sound knowledge of relevant economic concepts and principles with few, if any, errors			
Application (AO2)	effectively applied my knowledge of economics to the given context AND where appropriate, made good use of data to support my key points			
Analysis (AO3)	focused on developing a few key points that are relevant to the question AND developed my key points using clear, logical chains of reasoning			
Diagrams	if appropriate, included clear, accurately labelled diagrams AND referred to diagrams in the body of my response using symbols (e.g. P1, Q1)			

In addition to these areas, it is also important that you:

• respond to all parts of the set question

• use punctuation and grammar accurately

• complete your response within the time allowed (approximately 22.5 minutes)

Award yourself a mark out of 15

Level of response	Self-assessment	Max 15 marks
3	If you gave yourself mostly 3s	11–15 marks
2	If you gave yourself mostly 2s	6–10 marks
1	If you gave yourself mostly 1s	1–5 marks

Grade descriptors – 25-mark essay question

Self-assessment

Read your response and rate yourself on a scale of 1 to 3 for each of the descriptors below. Rate yourself 3 if you feel you have fulfilled the descriptor to a 'good' standard, 2 if to a 'reasonable' standard and 1 if to a 'limited' standard.

Assessment objectives (AO)	Descriptors	Self-ratings		
	In my written response, I have:	1	2	3
Organisation	used paragraphs to organise my ideas clearly and logically			
Knowledge (AO1)	used economic terminology appropriately with few, if any, errors AND shown a sound knowledge of relevant economic concepts and principles with few, if any, errors			
Application (AO2)	effectively applied my knowledge of economics to the given context AND where appropriate, made good use of data to support my key points			
Analysis (AO3)	focused on developing a few key points that are relevant to the question AND developed my key points using clear, logical chains of reasoning			
Evaluation (AO4)	demonstrated evaluation throughout my response using phrases like 'depends on' and 'however' AND justified my opinion in my conclusion by developing key points rather than simply repeating the points already made in the body of my essay			
Diagrams	if appropriate, included clear, accurately labelled diagrams AND referred to diagrams in the body of my response using symbols (e.g. P1, Q1)			

In addition to these areas, it is also important that you:

- respond to all parts of the set question
- use punctuation and grammar accurately
- complete your response within the time allowed (approximately 37.5 minutes)

Award yourself a mark out of 25

Level of response		Max 25 marks
5	Mostly 3s with well-supported evaluation throughout response	21–25 marks
4	Mostly 3s with some supported evaluation	16–20 marks
3	Mostly 3s but generally unsupported evaluation	11–15 marks
2	Mostly 2s	6–10 marks
1	Mostly 1s	1–5 marks

Grade descriptors – 10-mark essay question

Read your response and rate yourself on a scale of 1 to 3 for each of the descriptors below. Rate yourself 3 if you feel you have fulfilled the descriptor to a 'good' standard, 2 if to a 'reasonable' standard and 1 if to a 'limited' standard.

Assessment objectives (AO)	Descriptors In my written response, I have:	Self-ratings		
		1	2	3
Organisation	organised my ideas clearly and logically using paragraphs			
Knowledge (AO1)	included at least two relevant well-developed comparisons between UK trade with EU countries and UK trade and non-EU countries			
Application (AO2)	made effective use of data in Extract C to compare the importance of trade between the UK and EU countries and the UK and non-EU countries			
Analysis (AO3)	produced well-developed comparisons using clear, logical chains of reasoning			
Evaluation (AO4)	included a supported final judgement of the importance of trade between the UK and EU members compared with trade between the UK and non-EU member countries			

In addition to these areas, it is also important that you:

- respond to all parts of the set question

- use punctuation and grammar accurately

- complete your response within the time allowed (approximately 15 minutes)

Award yourself a mark out of 10

Level of response	Self-assessment	Max 10 marks
3	If you gave yourself mostly 3s	8–10 marks
2	If you gave yourself mostly 2s	4–7 marks
1	If you gave yourself mostly 1s	1–3 marks

A-level
Economics
Practice paper for AQA

Paper 1

Markets and market failure   Time allowed: 2 hours

Materials

For this paper you must have:
- some paper or a notepad for your answers
- a calculator.

Instructions
- Use black ink or black ball-point pen. Pencil should only be used for drawing.
- In **Section A**, answer **EITHER** Context 1 **OR** Context 2.
- In **Section B**, answer **one** essay.

Information
- There are 80 marks available on this paper.
- The marks for questions are shown in brackets.

Name: ....

Paper 1 Markets and market failure
DATA RESPONSE QUESTIONS

Section A

Answer EITHER Context 1 OR Context 2

Context 1 (Total for this context: 40 marks)

The UK tobacco market

Study **Extracts A, B and C** and then answer **all** parts of Context 1 that follow.

Extract A: Cigarette consumption in the UK, 1990–2014

Year	Price per pack (£)	Tax per pack (£)	Quantity consumed (billions of packs)
1990	1.65	1.20	5.13
1991	1.80	1.31	4.90
1992	2.08	1.55	4.64
1993	2.27	1.70	4.45
1994	2.52	1.93	4.42
1995	2.70	2.09	4.40
1996	2.89	2.26	4.36
1997	3.08	2.42	4.20
1998	3.36	2.65	4.20
1999	3.64	2.88	4.20
2000	3.88	3.08	4.08
2001	4.22	3.37	3.95
2002	4.39	3.46	3.80
2003	4.51	3.55	3.70
2004	4.65	3.65	3.60
2005	4.82	3.77	3.50
2006	5.05	3.91	3.38
2007	5.33	4.07	3.23
2008	5.44	4.18	3.08
2009	5.67	4.34	2.93
2010	6.13	4.67	2.63
2011	6.63	5.08	2.52
2012	7.09	5.45	2.30
2013	7.72	5.91	2.08
2014	8.23	6.25	1.99

Source: www.the-tma.org.uk

Extract B: The UK market for cigarettes

The cigarette and tobacco market in the UK is dominated by two companies, Imperial Tobacco Group (ITG) and Japan Tobacco International (JTI) which between them control approximately 84% of the market.

After peaking in 1974, UK sales of cigarettes and other tobacco products have declined steadily
5 over time. In recent years there has been a decline in the sale of premium tobacco brands and a corresponding growth in economy-priced cigarettes, roll-your-own (RYO) and electronic cigarettes. Economy-priced cigarettes now account for more than half of all cigarettes sold in the UK.

However, despite this decline in sales of manufactured cigarettes, the profits of the tobacco industry have not fallen. In 2009, the combined profit of the four companies with 94% of UK market share – ITG,
10 JTI, Philip Morris International (PMI) and British American Tobacco (BAT) – was more than £1 billion.

UK demand for electronic cigarettes (e-cigarettes) has risen dramatically in recent years, with annual sales estimated to be worth £126.8m. All of the major tobacco companies have invested in the development of electronic cigarettes or similar nicotine delivery devices and all now have products on sale in the UK.

Extract C: Regulation of the tobacco industry in the UK

In June 2016, new regulations came into effect in the UK forcing tobacco manufacturers to use standardised, plain packaging for cigarettes with 65% of the casing covered with text and images warning consumers of the harmful effects of cigarettes on their health.

Cigarette manufacturers were also told to get rid of any misleading information from cigarette packs,
5 and were prevented from using words such as 'organic', 'natural' or 'lite', which may lead consumers to believe there is a healthy smoking option.

The new regulations were an attempt to reduce the uptake of smoking, especially amongst young people. More than 600 young people were taking up smoking per day at the time these regulations were introduced.

10 In addition to this, the UK government also increased indirect taxes on cigarettes and other tobacco products in 2016. According to the World Health Organisation (WHO), the most effective option for governments in controlling the consumption of cigarettes is 'the simple elevation of tobacco prices by use of consumption taxes'.

The WHO claims that, on average, a 10% price increase on a pack of cigarettes would be expected to
15 reduce consumption of cigarettes by about 4% in high-income countries, such as the UK. They go on to recommend that governments set indirect taxes on tobacco products at more than 70% of the final consumer price.

Other measures the government has introduced to reduce cigarette consumption include bans on tobacco sales to those under 18 years of age, advertising bans, public smoking prohibitions and
20 provision of support, such as helplines, for those trying to give up smoking.

QUESTION 1

Using the data in **Extract A**, calculate, to two decimal places, the overall percentage increase in the price of cigarettes between 1990 and 2014.

[2 Marks]

QUESTION 2

Explain whether the data in **Extract A** confirms a normal demand curve relationship between price and the quantity of cigarettes consumed.

[4 Marks]

QUESTION 3

Extract B (lines 4–5) states that 'sales of cigarettes and other tobacco products have declined steadily over time'.

With the help of a diagram, explain the factors other than price that may have contributed to a fall in the demand for cigarettes.

[9 Marks]

QUESTION 4

In **Extract C**, (lines 11–13) the World Health Organisation suggests that the most effective option for governments in controlling the consumption of cigarettes is 'the simple elevation of tobacco prices by use of consumption taxes'.

Using data in the extracts and your economic knowledge, assess whether you agree that high indirect taxes on cigarettes are the best way to reduce the consumption of cigarettes and correct for market failure.

[25 Marks]

Context 2 (Total for this context: 40 marks)

The UK labour market

Study **Extracts D, E and F** and then answer **all** parts of Context 2 that follow.

Extract D: Trade union membership in the UK

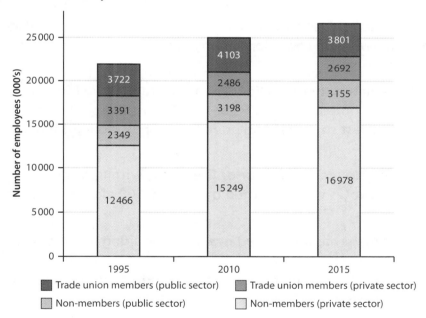

Extract E: UK government's changes to trade union laws

In 2016, the UK government introduced the Trade Union Act 2016 designed to restrict the powers of trade unions.

The new changes made strikes unlawful unless at least 50% of those being asked to strike voted in the ballot. There is also the requirement that, in key public services such as education, health, fire,
5 transport, border security and energy sectors, at least 40% of those asked to vote supported the strike action. For example, if 100 teachers were asked to strike, the action would only be lawful if at least 50 teachers voted and at least 40 backed the strike.

Other changes included the following:

- Unions must give at least 2 weeks' notice to the employer before the industrial action starts.
10 - Pickets and protests must have an identifiable and authorised supervisor.
- Regulators have the power to impose fines on unions of up to £20,000 for breaching rules.

The number of working days lost in the UK due to strikes was 704,000 in the 12 months to April 2015. This, however, is significantly less than the near 13 million days lost through strike action on average in the 1970s.

15 By limiting the powers of trade unions to take strike action, the government is restricting their ability to negotiate more favourable wages and working conditions, which should lead to lower unemployment. In contrast, strong trade union power is thought to raise the wage bill for employers, resulting in job losses.

The new laws may also lead to gains in productivity due to fewer lost working days from industrial
20 action and less disruption for the general public.

Extract F: Teachers' strike closes thousands of schools across England

On Tuesday 5 July 2016, the National Union of Teachers (NUT), the UK's largest trade union for teachers, took strike action against the government leaving an estimated 7,000 of England's 22,000 state schools closed or partially closed for a day. Teachers held rallies across England, with large turnouts in central London, Manchester and Brighton.

5 The NUT demanded an increase in funding to schools, arguing that funding cuts could led to an increase in class sizes, fewer subject choices for children and teacher redundancies. They also demanded negotiations on teacher contracts to allow pay and workload to be addressed. The NUT warned that unless pay and working conditions improve, the teacher recruitment and retention 'crisis' will not get better anytime soon.

10 In response to the NUT's demands, the then Education Secretary, Nicky Morgan, said there was no alternative to the pressure on teachers' pay. She said: 'across the public sector we have had to take difficult decisions in the last six years. And public sector pay is one of the areas that has been impacted'.

NUT members voted overwhelmingly in favour of the strike, with about 92% supporting the move.
15 However, only about 50,000 votes were returned by the 210,000 members balloted, a turnout of just 24%.

Since the strike, the government has introduced new laws requiring at least 50% of members entitled to vote to do so before industrial action can legally be taken. This will make it more difficult for teachers to launch strike action in the future. The government employs over 438,000 full-time
20 teachers in state-funded schools across England.

QUESTION 5

Using the data in **Extract D**, calculate, to two decimal places, the percentage of workers who belonged to a trade union in 1995 compared with 2015.

[2 marks]

QUESTION 6

Explain how the data in **Extract D** shows that trade unions in the public sector might be more successful in negotiating improved working conditions with their employer than trade unions in the private sector.

[4 marks]

QUESTION 7

Extract F (lines 7–9) states that 'The NUT warned that unless pay and working conditions improve, the teacher recruitment and retention 'crisis' will not get better anytime soon.'

With the help of a diagram, explain how the existence of a trade union could affect the supply of labour for teachers.

[9 marks]

QUESTION 8

Extract E (lines 17–18) states that 'strong trade union power is thought to raise the wage bill for employers, resulting in job losses'.

Using data in the extracts and your economic knowledge, assess the view that 'a trade union might be able to achieve higher wages for workers, but only by creating some unemployment'.

[25 marks]

Paper 1 – Section B

Answer **one** essay from this section.

Each essay carries 40 marks.

EITHER

Essay 1

> Tesco, the UK's largest supermarket chain, posted a pre-tax profit of £162m in 2016, a dramatic turnaround from the £6.4bn loss it posted in 2015. Chief Executive, Dave Lewis, said Tesco had regained competitiveness in the UK by offering customers 'significantly better service, a simpler range and lower and more stable prices' compared to its rivals.

QUESTION 9

Explain how a firm such as Tesco might try to increase its profits.

[15 marks]

QUESTION 10

Discuss the view that oligopolistic market structures, such as the supermarket industry in the UK, are good for consumers.

[25 marks]

OR

Essay 2

In the UK in 2016, 13 million people were living without enough income to meet their needs.

QUESTION 11

Explain how it is possible for relative and absolute poverty to exist in the UK.

[15 marks]

QUESTION 12

In 2016, the UK government introduced the National Living Wage (NLW), a new national minimum wage of £7.20 per hour for everyone 25 years old and over. The new rate was an increase of 50p on the previous minimum wage of £6.70. For those aged 21 to 25, however, the lower rate of £6.70 still applied.

Assess the view that the introduction of the National Living Wage is the best way to alleviate poverty in the UK.

[25 marks]

OR

Essay 3

In 2010, an explosion on the Deepwater Horizon oil drilling rig leased by oil giant BP sent millions of barrels of oil into the Gulf of Mexico. The spill had a devastating effect on the environment, wildlife and the fishing industry. BP was fined a record $20.8 billion (£15.6 billion) by the US government. The fine was used to compensate those affected by the spill and to restore the environment.

QUESTION 13

With the help of a diagram, explain why, without government intervention, the Deepwater Horizon oil spill is an example of market failure.

[15 marks]

QUESTION 14

Discuss the view that it is only possible to achieve economic efficiency through government intervention.

[25 marks]

Mark scheme for Paper 1 – Section A

Context 1

QUESTION 1

Using the data in **Extract A**, calculate, to two decimal places, the overall percentage increase in the price of cigarettes between 1990 and 2014.

[2 Marks]

Self-assessment

In order to gain two marks for this answer, you need to:	Achieved	Area for development
• calculate the answer correctly showing formula		
• express the answer as a percentage (%)		
• round the answer to two decimal places		

Award yourself a mark

• Incorrect answer (0 marks)

• Correct answer but not expressed as a percentage and/or rounded to two decimal places (1 mark)

• Correct answer expressed as a percentage and rounded to two decimal places (2 marks)

Example response

The price of a pack of cigarettes rose from £1.65 in 1990 to £8.23 in 2014.

The percentage increase was: $\dfrac{P1 - P0}{P0} \times 100 = \dfrac{£8.23 - £1.65}{£1.65} \times 100$

$$= 398.78\%$$

QUESTION 2

Explain whether the data in **Extract A** confirms a normal demand curve relationship between price and the quantity of cigarettes consumed.

[4 Marks]

Self-assessment

In order to gain four marks for this question, you need to:	Achieved	Area for development
• explain what a normal demand curve relationship is		
• use evidence to show that the price and quantity of cigarettes confirms a normal demand curve relationship		
• explain how the data is evidence of a normal demand curve relationship		
• explain how the data is not evidence of a normal demand curve relationship		

Award yourself a mark

Award yourself 1 mark for achieving each of the above criteria.

Example response

A normal demand curve relationship exists when an increase in price leads to a fall in quantity demanded (1 mark). Overall, the data confirms a normal demand curve relationship between price and quantity demanded (1 mark). As the price of cigarettes rose from £1.65 in 1990 to £8.23 in 2014, the consumption of cigarettes generally fell from about 5bn to 2bn packs (1 mark). However, the demand curve relationship is not normal between 1997 and 1999 when the consumption of cigarettes remained constant at about 4.2bn packs despite an increase in price from £3.08 to £3.64 over this period (1 mark).

QUESTION 3

Extract B (lines 4–5) states that 'sales of cigarettes and other tobacco products have declined steadily over time'.

With the help of a diagram, explain the factors other than price that may have contributed to a fall in the demand for cigarettes.

[9 Marks]

Self-assessment

Self-assess your response using the grade descriptors and levels of response on pages 9 and 15–19.

Example response

Analyse the example response below and consider how each of the grade descriptors is achieved using the annotations in the right hand column to help you. Go back and review your answer after analysing this response.

Demand is the quantity of a good or service that consumers are willing and able to buy at different prices over a period of time. A fall in the demand for cigarettes is shown by a shift to the left of the demand curve from D1 to D2 in fig. 1, resulting in a fall in price from P1 to P2 and a fall in the quantity traded from Q1 to Q2.

> AO1: Shows sound knowledge of the meaning of the term 'demand' and the effect of a fall in the demand for cigarettes.

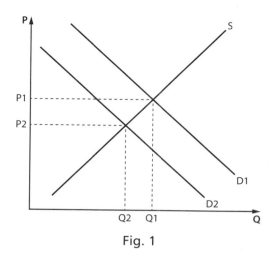

Fig. 1

The demand for cigarettes may fall due to a fall in the price of substitutes, such as e-cigarettes. A fall in the price of e-cigarettes may result in more smokers substituting e-cigarettes for traditional cigarettes, thereby leading to a fall in demand for traditional cigarettes. The cross-elasticity of demand (XED) is therefore likely to be positive. As e-cigarettes and traditional cigarettes are close substitutes, XED is likely to be elastic indicating that a fall in the price of e-cigarettes may lead to a proportionately larger fall in the quantity of cigarettes consumed. The price of e-cigarettes may have fallen due to increased competition in the e-cigarette market, with all major tobacco companies now selling e-cigarettes in the UK.

Demand for cigarettes may also have fallen due to legal controls on cigarette advertising. With limited exposure to cigarette advertisements, consumers are less likely to be persuaded to take up smoking, thereby reducing demand for cigarettes.

Fashion and tastes may also affect demand for cigarettes. As consumers become more aware of the harmful effects of cigarettes on their health, many are choosing to quit smoking, thereby reducing demand for cigarettes. Laws introduced by the government banning smoking in public places may also contribute to reduced consumption of cigarettes.

Other areas for discussion:

- During periods of economic recession when incomes are falling, demand for cigarettes may fall as people are less able to afford them (in other words, cigarettes are a normal good).

- Changing social attitudes towards smoking.

- Government campaigns that increase consumers' awareness of the harmful effects of smoking.

- The Behavioural Insights Team (BIT) role in making e-cigarettes available in the UK.

- BIT's use of nudge theory, e.g. simplifying the government 'quit smoking' website and encouraging smokers to try e-cigarettes.

> **AO3:** Logical chain of reasoning explaining the link between the price of e-cigarettes and the demand for traditional cigarettes.

> **AO2:** Explicit reference to Extract B. The entire response has also been applied to the context of the cigarette market in the UK.

- Availability of government helplines that support smokers in giving up.
- A fall in population may reduce demand for cigarettes.
- An increase in the price of complementary goods to cigarettes, e.g. alcohol.

LevelUP:	Rather than list a large number of points, it is best to choose the two most relevant points and develop them in detail. This is usually enough to score well in a 9-mark essay question. Remember to develop your points using logical chains of analysis and, where appropriate, use supporting data from the extracts.

Self-reflection

Think about your overall response to this question and note down at least one:

- **what went well** (WWW) – something you did well in your response
- **even better if** (EBI) – something you could have done better

Keep these points in mind and use them to improve your next attempt at an essay question.

QUESTION 4

In **Extract C**, (lines 11–13) the World Health Organisation suggests that the most effective option for governments in controlling the consumption of cigarettes is 'the simple elevation of tobacco prices by use of consumption taxes'.

Using data in the extracts and your economic knowledge, assess whether you agree that high indirect taxes on cigarettes are the best way to reduce the consumption of cigarettes and correct for market failure.

[25 Marks]

Self-assessment

Self-assess your response using the grade descriptors and levels of response on pages 9 and 15–19.

Example response

Market failure occurs when the market fails to allocate resources efficiently. A market is said to be allocatively efficient when the marginal social cost (MSC) is equal to the marginal social benefit (MSB), Q* in fig. 1 below.

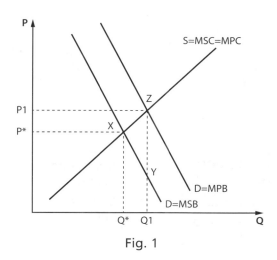

Fig. 1

Cigarettes are over-consumed in a free market as smokers base their consumption decisions on their private benefits and ignore the negative effects, such as health problems arising from second-hand smoke, on third parties. In fig. 1, the free market output of cigarettes is Q1, which is above the socially optimal output Q* and results in a deadweight loss to society of XYZ.

As a demerit good, cigarettes are also over-provided by the free market because of information failure, i.e. without government intervention, smokers do not fully understand the negative effects smoking has on their health and therefore consume more cigarettes than is optimal.

An indirect tax (a tax on expenditure) may be effective in reducing the consumption and production of cigarettes to the socially optimal level Q* in fig. 1. The imposition of an indirect tax on cigarettes would have the effect of increasing the cost of production, thereby shifting the supply curve to the left from S1 to S2, as shown in fig. 2 below. This would lead to an increase in price from P1 to P2 and a reduction in the quantity traded of cigarettes from Q1 to Q2.

AO1: Shows good understanding of the causes of market failure in the cigarette industry.

AO3: Logical chain of analysis explaining the impact of an indirect tax on the quantity of cigarettes traded.

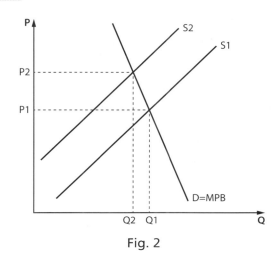

Fig. 2

Extract A provides evidence to support the view that higher taxes lead to reduced consumption of cigarettes. As the tax per pack rose from £1.20 in 1990 to £6.25 in 2014, consumption dropped from 5.13 billion to 1.99 billion packs per year. However, there may have been other factors that contributed to this fall in consumption such as a trend towards healthier lifestyle choices.

AO2: Application of data from Extract A.

The effectiveness of a tax in reducing cigarette consumption also depends upon the price elasticity of demand (PED) for the product. Demand for cigarettes is likely to be price inelastic as they are addictive and there are few close substitutes available. An increase in the price of cigarettes is therefore likely to lead to a proportionately smaller decrease in the quantity of cigarettes consumed, thereby limiting the effectiveness of an indirect tax in reducing cigarette consumption.

AO4: Comment evaluating the effect of an indirect tax on cigarette consumption in terms of PED.

The effectiveness of the tax would also depend on the government's ability to accurately estimate the external costs of cigarette consumption which is difficult to measure in monetary terms. In fig. 1, the indirect tax must be equal to the distance ZY in order to fully internalise the external cost of cigarette consumption and reduce output to the socially optimal level, Q*. An indirect tax which is too high or too low will fail to achieve Q*, resulting in a welfare loss to society.

AO4: Paragraph evaluating the effect of an indirect tax on cigarette consumption in terms of the amount of the tax.

Another problem with an indirect tax is that it does not correct for information failure on the part of consumers. Awareness campaigns designed to educate young people on the harmful effects of smoking may help to reduce the number of young people taking up smoking each day to below 600. The effectiveness of these campaigns, however, would depend on how successful the government is at targeting young people and getting the message across.

AO4: Comment evaluating the effectiveness of awareness campaigns designed to reduce smoking.

The UK government could also modify the behaviour of smokers using nudge theory. One example of this is the work of the Behavioural Insights Team (BIT) which has been effective in encouraging smokers to switch to the less harmful e-cigarettes.

The UK government's law forcing cigarette companies to use plain unbranded packaging for cigarettes, with warnings to consumers, could correct for information failure, thereby decreasing demand for cigarettes and reducing output to a more efficient level. However, the effectiveness of this measure would depend on the government's ability to monitor cigarette companies to ensure they are complying with the new law.

In conclusion, while the imposition of an indirect tax is an effective way of reducing the consumption of cigarettes and correcting for market failure, I do not think it is the 'best' way. As well as problems associated with setting the tax at an appropriate level, an indirect tax is regressive meaning it impacts low income consumers more than high income consumers, thereby worsening inequality. I think the best approach would be to generate awareness of the harmful effects of cigarettes, especially amongst young people, perhaps using nudge theory, in order to correct for information failure, one of the root causes of cigarette over-consumption.

AO4: Opinion stated followed by clear justification which considers the effect of indirect taxes on inequality rather than simply repeating points already mentioned in the body of the response.

Other areas for discussion:

- PED can be calculated as –0.4 for developed countries using data from Extract C.

- An advantage of a tax is that it generates revenue for the government.

- Tax revenue could also be used to set up telephone helplines that smokers can call for support to give up smoking.

- An indirect tax has the advantage of utilising the market mechanism to adjust output to the social optimal level, unlike measures such as price controls that may result in a disequilibrium in the market.

- Legal controls such as bans on advertising and legal age limits on who can purchase cigarettes could also be effective in reducing cigarette consumption.

LevelUP: When writing your conclusion, avoid simply repeating points already made in the body of your response. Mentioning the same point repeatedly will not gain you additional marks. You must show you can analyse and evaluate by developing these points in some way. The best way to do this is to make a judgement on which of the points is the most significant in relation to the question.

Self-reflection

Think about your overall response to this question and note down at least one:

- **what went well** (WWW) – something you did well in your response

- **even better if** (EBI) – something you could have done better

Keep these points in mind and use them to improve your next attempt at an essay question.

Context 2

QUESTION 5

Using the data in **Extract D**, calculate, to two decimal places, the percentage of workers who belonged to a trade union in 1995 compared with 2015.

[2 Marks]

Self-assessment

In order to gain two marks for this answer, you need to:	Achieved	Area for development
• calculate the answer correctly		
• express the answer as a percentage (%)		
• round the answer to two decimal places		

Award yourself a mark

- Incorrect answer (0 marks)

- Correct answer but not expressed as a percentage and/or rounded to two decimal places (1 mark)

- Correct answer expressed as a percentage and rounded to two decimal places (2 marks)

Example response

1995: $\dfrac{3{,}722 + 3{,}391}{3{,}722 + 3{,}391 + 2{,}349 + 12{,}466} \times 100 = \dfrac{7{,}113}{21{,}928} \times 100 = \mathbf{32.44\%}$

2015: $\dfrac{3{,}801 + 2{,}692}{3{,}801 + 2{,}692 + 3{,}155 + 16{,}978} \times 100 = \dfrac{6{,}493}{26{,}626} \times 100 = \mathbf{24.39\%}$

32.44% (1 mark) of workers belonged to a trade union in 1995 compared with **24.39%** (1 mark) in 2015.

2 marks possible without workings (BUT, always show your workings!)

QUESTION 6

Explain how the data in **Extract D** shows that trade unions in the public sector might be more successful in negotiating improved working conditions with their employer than trade unions in the private sector.

[4 Marks]

Self-assessment

In order to gain four marks for this question, you need to:	Achieved	Area for development
• explain 'strength in numbers'		
• explain how the data is evidence that public sector union members have more power to bargain collectively		
• explain how the data is evidence that private sector union members have less power to bargain collectively		
• link evidence back to the question		

Award yourself a mark

Award yourself 1 mark for achieving each of the above criteria.

Example response

A trade union's ability to successfully negotiate improved working conditions depends on its power to bargain with its employer (1 mark). Well over 50% of public sector workers were members of a trade union in all years (1 mark). In contrast, the proportion of private sector workers who belonged to a trade union was below 20% in all years (1 mark). Through strength in numbers (collective bargaining) and the threat of industrial action (1 mark), public sector workers may be more able to put pressure on the government to improve pay and working conditions.

QUESTION 7

Extract F (lines 7–9) states that 'The NUT warned that unless pay and working conditions improve, the teacher recruitment and retention 'crisis' will not get better anytime soon.'

With the help of a diagram, explain how the existence of a trade union could affect the supply of labour for teachers.

[9 Marks]

Self-assessment

Self-assess your response using the grade descriptors and levels of response on pages 9 and 15–19.

Example response

The supply of labour is the ability and willingness of workers to provide (i.e. supply) their labour at different wage rates. The factors affecting labour supply include the wage rate and non-wage benefits in the industry, the wages in alternative occupations and changes in the working population.

A trade union is an organisation that represents the interests of employees. Through the power of collective bargaining, trade unions have the potential to affect the factors influencing labour supply. For example, as members of a trade union, workers are in a better position to negotiate higher wages through collective bargaining with employers and the threat of industrial action, increasing wages from w1 to w2 but reducing the number of workers employed from L1 to L2 in fig. 1.

AO1: Shows knowledge and understanding of the economic theory of trade unions.

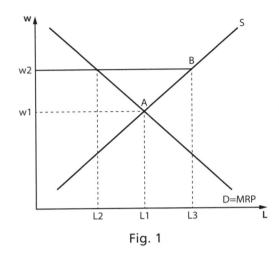

Fig. 1

If the NUT are successfully able to negotiate higher wages for teachers, the wage teachers receive will be higher relative to other professions. This may encourage workers into teaching from other occupations, leading to an increase in the number of teachers willing and able to supply their labour, resulting in a movement along the supply curve from points A to B in fig. 1.

AO3: Clear chain of analysis linking higher wages for teachers to an increase in the number of individuals willing to supply their labour in the industry. Reference to the diagram helps to clarify explanation.

An improvement in non-wage benefits as a result of trade union negotiations may also attract more workers into the profession, leading to an increase in the supply of teachers and shifting the labour supply curve for teachers outward to the left from S1 to S2 as shown in fig. 2 below. For example, a reduction in workload, improved holidays or improved pension schemes may result in more individuals taking up teaching.

AO2: Application achieved by providing examples within the context of the teaching industry.

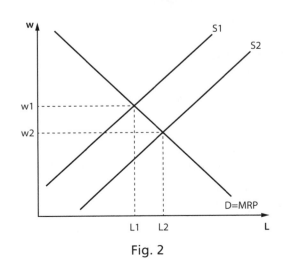

Fig. 2

On the other hand, if the NUT are unsuccessful in their negotiations, lower wages and worsening non-wage benefits for teachers relative to other professions may result in teachers leaving the industry for more favourable pay and conditions in other industries. This could explain the 'recruitment and retention crisis' mentioned in Extract F.

AO2: Application to the information contained in Extract F.

Other areas for discussion:

- The income and substitution effects leading to the backward bending labour supply curve for an individual.

- The NUT could restrict the supply of teachers by requiring certain qualifications, thereby shifting the supply curve to the left.

LevelUP: Take the time to practise drawing diagrams in preparation for your exams. You should aim to produce diagrams in under a minute. Remember, diagrams should be about one third of a page in size and MUST be clearly labelled.

Self-reflection

Think about your overall response to this question and note down at least one:

- **what went well** (WWW) – something you did well in your response

- **even better if** (EBI) – something you could have done better

Keep these points in mind and use them to improve your next attempt at an essay question.

QUESTION 8

Extract E (lines 17–18) states that 'strong trade union power is thought to raise the wage bill for employers, resulting in job losses'.

Using data in the extracts and your economic knowledge, assess the view that 'a trade union might be able to achieve higher wages for workers, but only by creating some unemployment'.

[25 Marks]

Self-assessment

Self-assess your response using the grade descriptors and levels of response on pages 9 and 15–19.

Example response

A perfectly competitive labour market is a market in which there are many buyers (employers) and sellers (employees) of labour, perfect mobility of labour, firms and workers must accept the market wage and firms seek to maximise profits.

In a perfectly competitive labour market, firms will employ workers up to the point where wage equals MRP (w = MRP). Thus, at a wage of w1 in fig. 1 the firm will employ N1 workers, where w = MRP. It would not be profitable for the firm to employ N1 + 1 workers as the additional cost of the worker (w1) would be greater than the additional revenue (MRP) the worker would generate for the firm.

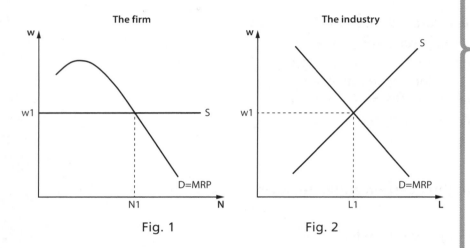

Fig. 1   Fig. 2

AO1: Shows good understanding of the economic theory of wage determination in a perfectly competitive labour market.

In this example, firms must pay the industry wage, w1 in fig. 2, which is determined by the intersection of the labour demand or MRP curve (D = MRP) and the labour supply curve (S) in the industry. At this wage L1 workers are employed in the industry.

However, the existence of a trade union (an organisation set up to protect the interests of workers) is a market imperfection which enables workers to bargain collectively for higher wages and improved working conditions, behaving like a single seller of labour.

Through the threat of industrial action, trade unions have the power to bargain up wages paid by employers, increasing wage from w1 to w2 in fig. 3. The new wage, w2, is above the perfectly competitive equilibrium wage, w1. The effect of this is a fall in the number of workers employed in the industry from L1 to L2 and unemployment of L2L3 in fig. 3.

AO3: Logical chain of reasoning linking trade unions to the possibility of higher unemployment.

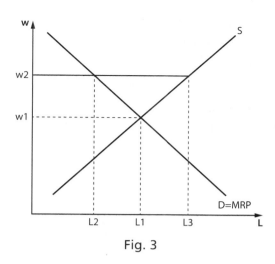

Fig. 3

Thus, according to economic theory, the existence of trade unions can lead to higher wages and unemployment in an industry. The extent of this unemployment, however, would depend on the elasticity of demand and elasticity supply of labour in the industry. Due to the specialist skills and qualifications needed to teach in the UK, teaching is likely to have relatively inelastic supply. Similarly, demand for teachers is likely to be relatively inelastic due to the essential nature of the product (education) thus minimising, but not eliminating, the effect on unemployment.

> **AO4:** A comment evaluating the factors affecting the extent of unemployment caused by trade unions.

However, this may not be the case in an industry that has a monopsony employer of workers. A monopsony is a market imperfection in which there is a single buyer of labour. A monopsony has the effect of driving down wages as shown in fig. 4.

> **AO4:** Comment foregrounding an evaluative discussion on the effect of trade unions on unemployment in an industry in which there is a monopsony employer of labour.

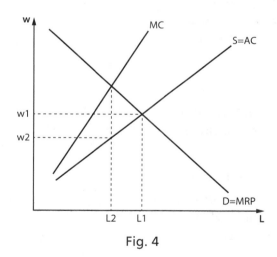

Fig. 4

The UK government employs over 438,000 teachers in state schools, giving it significant monopsony power.

> **AO2:** Application of data from Extract F.

As a monopsony is the only buyer of labour in the industry, it faces an upward sloping labour supply curve, S = AC. The firm will maximise profits by employing workers up to the point where MC = MRP. At this point, the firm pays a wage of w2 and employs L2 workers. Thus, the effect of a monopsony is to drive down wage from w1 to w2 and reduce the number of workers employed from L1 to L2.

The existence of a trade union in an industry which is dominated by a monopsony employer, such as in teaching, can counter the effect of the monopsony by raising wages and also raising the level of employment.

The introduction of a trade union such as the NUT would be to increase the wage from w2 to w3 and increase the level of employment from L2 to L3 as shown in fig. 5.

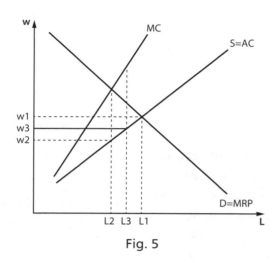

Fig. 5

In conclusion, whether or not unemployment will be created by a trade union achieving higher wages depends on the industry. In teaching, as the government is a monopsony employer of teachers, higher wages negotiated by the NUT may lead to higher rather than lower levels of employment in the industry. However, in industries that are not dominated by monopsony employers, higher wages may indeed lead to some unemployment. The extent of this would depend on elasticities of demand and supply of labour in the industry.

Other areas for discussion:

- The NUT's ability to increase wages and increase employment in the industry depends on teachers' willingness to take industrial action – under 25% of teachers voted in the ballot.

- Other factors affecting the power of trade unions to bargain up wages, including: the proportion of employees in the industry who are members of the trade union, the profitability of the employer and labour costs as a proportion of total costs in the industry.

- New laws imposed by the government would have made the July 5th strike unlawful, reducing the NUT's ability to achieve higher wages.

Self-reflection

Think about your overall response to this question and note down at least one:

- **what went well** (WWW) – something you did well in your response

- **even better if** (EBI) – something you could have done better

Keep these points in mind and use them to improve your next attempt at an essay question.

Mark scheme for Paper 1 – Section B

Essay 1

> Tesco, the UK's largest supermarket chain, posted a pre-tax profit of £162m in 2016, a dramatic turnaround from the £6.4bn loss it posted in 2015. Chief Executive, Dave Lewis, said Tesco had regained competitiveness in the UK by offering customers 'significantly better service, a simpler range and lower and more stable prices' compared to its rivals.

QUESTION 9

Explain how a firm such as Tesco might try to increase its profits.

[15 Marks]

Self-assessment

Self-assess your response using the grade descriptors and levels of response on pages 9 and 15–19.

Example response

Profit is the difference between total revenue (TR) and total cost (TC). A firm seeking to maximise profit will operate at the level of output where marginal cost (MC) equals marginal revenue (MR).

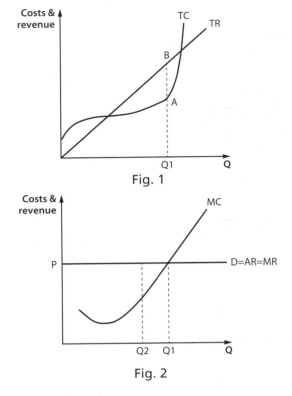

Fig. 1

Fig. 2

MC is the additional cost of producing an additional unit of output. MR is the additional revenue generated from that additional unit of output. At output Q2 in fig. 2, MR is greater than MC indicating that there is still profit to be gained from producing an additional unit. Profit is therefore maximised when MC = MR at Q1. At Q1 the distance between the TR and TC curves in fig. 1, AB, is maximised.

> **AO1:** Shows a good understanding of the MC = MR profit maximising condition.

A firm such as Tesco could increase its profit by either increasing TR or reducing TC.

It may be possible for Tesco to increase TR by changing price. The effect of a change in price on TR depends on price elasticity of demand (PED). As Tesco's products have a large number of substitutes available from competitors such as Asda and Sainsbury, PED is likely to be elastic. Hence, 'lower more stable prices' may lead to an increase in Tesco's TR and profit.

> **AO2:** Application through reference to Tesco's competitors. This paragraph also shows good knowledge, analysis and, even though it is not required for a 9-mark question, evaluation.

Another way of increasing TR is through non-price competition such as advertising to attract customers. As well as increasing sales of Tesco's products and hence TR, effective advertising may also help Tesco to create a stronger brand. This would make the PED for Tesco's products more inelastic, enabling them to increase TR by charging higher prices in the future. However, the overall effect of advertising on profit will depend on the cost of the advertising campaign. If the cost of advertising exceeds the additional revenue generated from the increase in sales, TR and profit will fall rather than rise.

Tesco could also increase profitability by reducing costs. This could be done by lowering wages or by replacing workers with technology, e.g. self-service checkout counters, which may reduce TC and increase profit. As Tesco is a large company, it may also be able

> **AO3:** Logical chain of reasoning explaining the link between lower costs and higher profit.

to negotiate bulk discounts with suppliers (purchasing economies) reducing unit cost and increasing profit. Tesco could also reduce costs by closing unprofitable stores, thereby increasing profit.

Other points for discussion:

- As Tesco operates in an oligopolistic market structure, profits could be boosted through price fixing (collusion with competitors). However, this would be illegal.

- Tesco could enter a price war with competitors in an attempt to eliminate competition by driving them out of the market (predatory pricing), although this would be illegal. While profits will fall in the short run, long-run profits may rise as a result of reduced competition.

- Tesco could sell assets (including those in other countries) in order to cover losses, repay debt and boost profitability.

- Profits could be increased though the use of price discrimination, i.e. charging different groups of consumers different prices depending on the respective price elasticities of demand. One example of this might be the opening of 'Tesco Express' stores in city centres that charge customers higher prices for products.

> **LevelUP:** It's good practice to start your essay responses by defining the key economic term(s) in the question and outlining the relevant economic theory. This ensures that you demonstrate knowledge (AO1) early in your response and also helps you to focus in on the central economic idea of the question.

Self-reflection

Think about your overall response to this question and note down at least one:

- **what went well** (WWW) – something you did well in your response

- **even better if** (EBI) – something you could have done better

Keep these points in mind and use them to improve your next attempt at an essay question.

QUESTION 10

Discuss the view that the oligopolistic market structures, such as the supermarket industry in the UK, are good for consumers.

[25 Marks]

Self-assessment

Self-assess your response using the grade descriptors and levels of response on pages 9 and 15–19.

Example response

An oligopoly is a market structure in which there are a few large firms and high barriers to entry. There is interdependence between firms and they seek to maximise profits by operating at MC = MR. Whether or not an oligopolistic market structure is good for consumers depends on the behaviour of the firms.

In a competitive oligopoly, prices tend to be rigid due to the interdependence between firms. This can be explained by the kinked demand curve theory.

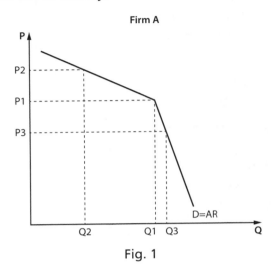

Fig. 1

If firm A in fig. 1 increases price from P1 to P2, other firms will respond by keeping prices unchanged. Firm A will therefore lose market share and total revenue will fall. On the other hand, if firm A decreases price from P1 to P3, other firms will respond by reducing their prices also in order to maintain their market share. This will also lead to a fall in firm A's total revenue. Hence, the best option is for firm A and other firms in the industry to leave their prices unchanged at P1.

AO1: Shows a good understanding of the kinked demand curve.

As a result of this, firms in oligopolistic markets tend to compete using non-price methods of competition, such as improved customer service and promotional offers. It is therefore possible for customers to benefit from better service, such as free delivery of groceries to their homes, and promotional offers, such as 'buy one get one free'. Non-price competition amongst firms may also lead to a greater range of products and more choice for consumers.

AO2: Application to the context of the supermarket industry.

As well as non-price competition, Tesco has also lowered the price of some of its products, thus benefiting consumers with cheaper groceries. Many oligopolistic firms, however, may be reluctant to do this as it may lead to lower revenue and profits as explained by the kinked demand curve theory above. It may also lead to a price war which, while beneficial for customers in the short run due to lower prices, may drive competitors out of the market, potentially leading to less choice and higher prices in the long run.

AO4: The decision to lower prices evaluated in terms of how other firms might respond and short-run versus long-run consequences.

In 2016, Tesco made a pre-tax profit of £162m. High profits such as this could be used by Tesco to improve dynamic efficiency within the firm, thus benefiting consumers. For example, retained profit could be used to create new products (product innovation) or be invested in the development of new technology leading to lower unit production costs which may result in lower prices for consumers in the long run (process innovation).

AO1: Main points are clearly linked back to the question, i.e. the impact on consumers, in each paragraph.

On the other hand, consumers could be exploited if firms in an oligopolistic market colluded and formed a cartel. The cartel's profits would be maximised when the industry MR is equal to the industry MC, at price P1 and output Q1 in fig. 2 below. Acting like a monopoly, cartel members would have to agree to restrict output to Q1. This would result in deadweight loss to society of XYZ. By increasing price to P1 and restricting output to Q1, cartel members would be able to appropriate consumer surplus, turning it into producer surplus.

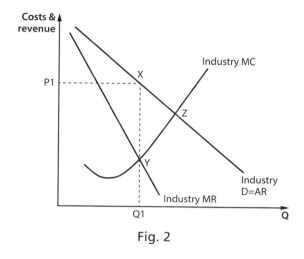

Fig. 2

However, collusion is illegal in the UK, with strict penalties such as fines in place to deter collusive behaviour. Despite this, collusion, especially tacit collusion, can be difficult for the government to detect and prove. This may result in consumers paying higher prices than necessary in some industries. Some cartel members, however, may use their profits to invest in research and development which could lead to improvements in the products available to consumers.

AO3: Logical chain of reasoning explaining the link between collusive behaviour by firms and the impact it has on the consumer.

In conclusion, provided the government is able to effectively discourage collusive behaviour, oligopolistic markets, like the UK supermarket industry, are generally good for consumers. The extent of this benefit to consumers will also depend on the degree of market contestability that exists in the industry. An oligopolistic market that is highly contestable due to the threat of new entrants, e.g. Walmart, is more likely to benefit consumers in the form of lower prices and increased choice.

AO4: Sentence evaluating the overall effect on consumers which develops, rather than simply repeats, previous points.

Other points for discussion:

- Collusion is only effective in industries where there are a small number of firms who trust each other. Consumers are less likely to suffer the negative effects of collusion in industries that do not exhibit these characteristics.

- Diagram showing the behaviour of a firm operating in a contestable market, i.e. making normal profit. This would benefit consumers with lower prices, thus increasing consumer surplus.

LevelUP: Try to support your main points with examples wherever possible as they help to develop and clarify your explanations. Depending on the question, examples can be taken from the context provided or from your own knowledge of the real world (AO2: Application).

Self-reflection

Think about your overall response to this question and note down at least one:

- **what went well** (WWW) – something you did well in your response
- **even better if** (EBI) – something you could have done better

Keep these points in mind and use them to improve your next attempt at an essay question.

Essay 2

In the UK in 2016, 13 million people were living without enough income to meet their needs.

QUESTION 11

Explain how it is possible for relative and absolute poverty to exist in the UK.

[15 Marks]

Self-assessment

Self-assess your response using the grade descriptors and levels of response on pages 9 and 15–19.

Example response

Relative poverty occurs when an individual cannot afford to participate in the normal activities of the society in which they live. In the UK, families who are unable to afford school uniforms for their children or an internet connection could be considered to be living in relative poverty. Absolute poverty occurs when individuals cannot afford basic necessities such as food, rent and clothing. According to the World Bank, individuals living on less than $1.90 a day are said to be living in extreme (absolute) poverty.

AO1: Definitions of the key economic terms in the question followed by examples show a clear understanding of the concepts.

The main cause of both relative and absolute poverty in the UK is unemployment. The unemployed are those who are actively seeking but unable to find paid work. If individuals are without employment or a stable income, they may not be able to afford to pay rent or buy essentials for their children leading to relative poverty. If they are unemployed over the longer term and without state support, they may not be able to afford the basic necessities like food and clothing, leading to absolute poverty.

AO3: Logical chain of analysis linking unemployment to relative poverty.

Another cause of poverty in the UK is low wages or insecure jobs. Unskilled, casual workers tend to earn very low wages, which may result in poverty, particularly if they are the main income earner for their family.

Additionally, individuals who have permanent disabilities or long-term sickness that prevent them from working may be dependent on state benefits and suffer from relative poverty. Some elderly pensioners who are dependent on state pensions may also fall into this low income, relative poverty, group.

Some individuals may also fall into the poverty trap, where the additional disposable income they receive from finding paid work is more than offset by the income they lose from reduced benefits and higher taxes. High housing and energy costs in the UK may also make it difficult for the unemployed or those on low incomes to escape relative poverty.

AO2: Reference to the context of the UK throughout the response is enough to gain marks for application.

In contrast to relative poverty, absolute poverty is rare in the UK due to the availability of state benefits for those most in need. However, it may be the case that individuals for some reason fail to claim the state benefits available to them, perhaps because they are unaware of what they are entitled to, leading to them living in absolute poverty.

Other points for discussion:

- High cost of child care, particularly for solo parents.

- Reference to the Gini coefficient as a measure of inequality – the Gini coefficient for disposable income in 2014/15 in the UK was 0.326 according to the Office for National Statistics.

- Zero-hour contracts may lead to increased poverty. Under zero-hour contracts, employers are not obligated to provide workers with any minimum working hours, which may result in long periods with no income.

- An ineffective benefit system may also result in some people not receiving the financial support they need.

- Some groups, such as asylum seekers, who are not permitted to work in the UK and receive minimal state support, may suffer from relative poverty.

Self-reflection

Think about your overall response to this question and note down at least one:

- **what went well** (WWW) – something you did well in your response
- **even better if** (EBI) – something you could have done better

Keep these points in mind and use them to improve your next attempt at an essay question.

QUESTION 12

In 2016, the UK government introduced the National Living Wage (NLW), a new national minimum wage of £7.20 per hour for everyone 25 years old and over. The new rate was an increase of 50p on the previous minimum wage of £6.70. For those aged 21 to 25, however, the lower rate of £6.70 still applied.

Assess the view that the introduction of the National Living Wage is the best way to alleviate poverty in the UK.

[25 Marks]

Self-assessment

Self-assess your response using the grade descriptors and levels of response on pages 9 and 15–19.

Example response

The NLW is an increase in the national minimum wage for everyone in the UK 25 years and over. The national minimum wage is a minimum hourly wage that must be paid to workers by employers.

According to economic theory, the effect of an increase in the national minimum wage would be to increase wages paid by employers from w1 to 'w min' and reduce the number of workers employed from L1 to L2 in fig. 1.

> **AO1:** Shows good knowledge of the economic theory relating to minimum wage.

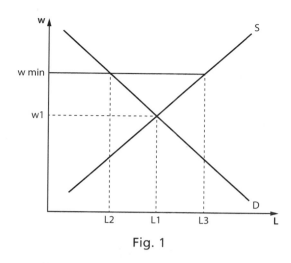

Fig. 1

This may help to alleviate poverty as a significant number of low skilled workers over the age of 25 are likely to experience an immediate increase in their disposable income as a result of the NLW. This will mean that they are able to afford an improved standard of living for themselves and their families.

AO2: Application to the context of the NLW, which is only available to those over the age of 25.

Workers already earning a wage above the NLW are also likely to receive a pay rise as employers seek to maintain existing pay differentials for those higher up the pay scale. As a result of higher incomes, consumer spending is likely to increase, leading to a multiplier effect on the creation of jobs and output, leading to economic growth.

AO3: Logical chain of analysis linking higher incomes with lower unemployment and higher economic growth.

The higher wage rate may also encourage employers to invest in training for their workers in order to make them more productive. More skilled workers will have improved job prospects and a better chance of escaping poverty. However, by making workers more productive, employers may require fewer workers, leading to redundancies. Those workers who are made redundant may fall into poverty, while those who keep their jobs have a better chance of escaping poverty.

AO4: Comment evaluating the impact of the higher NLW on different groups.

The NLW may not be effective in alleviating poverty for low skilled workers who have their hours and overtime cut as employers seek to reduce their wage bill. This may result in workers receiving the same or less weekly disposable income than previously. Also, only those aged 25 years and older will benefit directly from the NLW, with no direct wage increase for younger workers who may be living in poverty.

Furthermore, the introduction of the NLW may have the effect of increasing unemployment, L1L3 in fig. 1, as employers may seek to replace workers with machinery in the longer run. In low skilled jobs, where the elasticities of demand and supply for labour are likely to be relatively elastic, the effect of the higher NLW on unemployment is likely to be particularly significant. The extent of the unemployment will also depend on the rate at which the NLW is set. The higher the NLW is above the equilibrium wage, the greater will be the effect on unemployment. Higher unemployment is likely to lead to increased poverty.

AO4: Evaluation of the effect of the NLW on unemployment in terms of elasticities of demand and supply of labour and the extent of the wage increase relative to the equilibrium wage.

Employers may also seek to cover the higher wages resulting from the NLW by increasing prices, which may result in higher inflation and a fall in the real value of workers' incomes. This would have the effect of reducing the impact of the NLW and making goods and services even less affordable for those aged under 25 years of age who were not eligible for the NLW, and potentially worsening poverty.

As an alternative to the NLW, the government could aim to reduce unemployment using demand-side and supply-side policies, such as increasing the provision of education and training. Increasing progressive taxes and cutting regressive taxes may also help to distribute income more equally and alleviate poverty. Tax revenue raised from higher progressive taxes could be used to increase the provision of means tested state benefits more effectively, targeting those most in need, e.g. families with children and low single-income households. However, higher progressive taxes may create a disincentive to work and higher benefits may create a disincentive to find paid employment, leading to increased voluntary unemployment.

AO4: Paragraph evaluating policies to alleviate poverty other than the NLW.

While the introduction of the NLW may help to alleviate poverty for some individuals in the short term, it is not the 'best' way to tackle the problem over the longer term as it fails to target those most in need. The best approach in my opinion would be to focus on the root cause of the problem, unemployment. Over the long run, the UK government should focus on creating jobs and investing in training and education in order to make those without jobs more skilled and employable. In the short term, those affected by poverty could be targeted to receive financial support through government intervention such as means-tested benefits.

AO1: Explicit reference to the essay question in the conclusion.

Other areas for discussion:

- The introduction of the NLW will not help to alleviate poverty for those who are currently unemployed and may even make it harder for them to find jobs, especially if they are over 25 years old, as the cost of employing them will be higher.

- Younger workers below the age of 25 may indirectly benefit from the NLW as they will be relatively cheaper to employ, which may make it easier for them to find jobs.

- The NLW would help a worker who is the main income earner of their family more than one who has a partner or spouse who is also earning an income.

- The NLW offers a greater incentive to work, reducing voluntary unemployment. The higher NLW may also benefit those caught in the 'unemployment trap' – those who choose not to work as the income they would earn from working is not significantly higher than the state benefits they currently receive.

- The higher NLW may have a multiplier effect on consumption, leading to increased employment.

• The NLW does not effectively target those most in need. For example, many workers on low wages may be second wage earners in their household and may not be suffering the effects of poverty.

LevelUP: It is important, particularly in responses to 25-mark essay questions, that you demonstrate the skill of evaluation throughout your response. Remember, economic outcomes often depend on a range of factors. Be sure to demonstrate evaluation in your writing by explicitly considering these factors throughout your extended essay responses. A good sentence starter would be: 'The significance of <issue/concept> will depend on...'.

Self-reflection

Think about your overall response to this question and note down at least one:

• **what went well** (WWW) – something you did well in your response

• **even better if** (EBI) – something you could have done better

Keep these points in mind and use them to improve your next attempt at an essay question.

Essay 3

QUESTION 13

In 2010, an explosion on the Deepwater Horizon oil drilling rig leased by oil giant BP sent millions of barrels of oil into the Gulf of Mexico. The spill had a devastating effect on the environment, wildlife and the fishing industry. BP was fined a record $20.8 billion (£15.6 billion) by the US government. The fine was used to compensate those affected by the spill and to restore the environment.

With the help of a diagram, explain why, without government intervention, the Deepwater Horizon oil spill is an example of market failure.

[15 Marks]

Self-assessment

Self-assess your response using the grade descriptors and levels of response on pages 9 and 15–19.

Example response

Market failure occurs when the free market fails to allocate resources efficiently. One type of market failure is due to the existence of externalities. An externality occurs when a transaction between two individuals has a spill-over effect on a third party not directly involved in that transaction.

The Deepwater Horizon oil disaster is an example of a negative externality (or external cost) as it had a negative impact on third parties, i.e. the wildlife, environment and the fishing industry. It is a negative externality of production as it occurred in the production of oil for the consumer market.

> **AO2:** Application to the context of the exam question, i.e. the Deepwater Horizon oil spill.

With minimal government intervention, firms motivated by profit will base their production decisions on their private costs and ignore the external costs of production, leading to the product being overprovided by the market (market failure). The private costs to the oil firm are the costs directly incurred in the production of oil, e.g. the wages of oil workers. The social cost is the total cost to society, including both the costs to the individuals directly involved in the transaction (private costs) and the costs to the third parties (external costs).

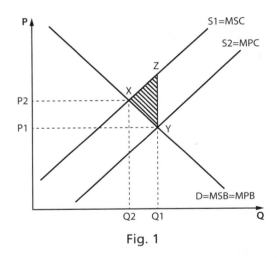

Fig. 1

In the market for oil, the free market equilibrium is price P1 and quantity Q1, where the marginal private cost (MPC) equals the marginal private benefit (MPB). Therefore, without government intervention, oil companies base their price and output decisions on their private costs and ignore the external costs of production due to the profit motive.

> **AO1:** Shows good understanding of the concept of negative externalities of production and the supporting diagram.

As a result, the production of oil is above the socially optimal output Q2, where the marginal social cost (MSC) equals the marginal social benefit (MSB). The free market has therefore provided more oil than is optimal for society resulting in a deadweight loss of XYZ. The Deepwater Horizon oil spill is an example of an external cost which, without intervention from the government, may have been ignored by the firm, BP, thereby leading to market failure.

> **AO3:** Logical chain of reasoning embedded in the economic theory of negative externalities of production with a clear link back to the question.

Other areas for discussion:

- The external cost is the difference between the social cost and the private cost.

> **LevelUP:** Remember, 'quality not quantity'. The response above is relatively short but covers all of the key points in the question. Writing more than is required doesn't directly lose you marks but it does cost you time… which means lost marks if you can't finish the paper.

Self-reflection

Think about your overall response to this question and note down at least one:

- **what went well** (WWW) – something you did well in your response
- **even better if** (EBI) – something you could have done better

Keep these points in mind and use them to improve your next attempt at an essay question.

QUESTION 14

Discuss the view that it is only possible to achieve economic efficiency through government intervention.

[25 Marks]

Self-assessment

Self-assess your response using the grade descriptors and levels of response on pages 9 and 15–19.

Example response

Economic efficiency exists when both productive and allocative efficiency are achieved. A firm is productively efficient when its average cost (AC) of production is minimised, point X at output Q1 in fig. 1. Allocative efficiency occurs when the right goods are produced in the right quantities thereby minimising waste. For a firm, the condition for allocative efficiency is price equals marginal cost (P = MC), point Y at output Q2 in fig. 2.

> **AO1:** Shows a clear understanding of productive and allocative efficiency.

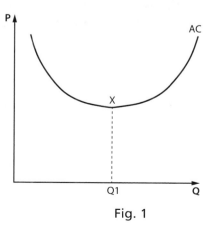

Fig. 1

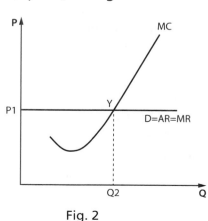

Fig. 2

Markets tend towards productive efficiency due to competition. Firms will seek to minimise average cost in order to remain competitive and profitable. Markets also tend towards allocative efficiency as the firms have an incentive to produce the right goods (the goods that consumers want) in the right quantities in order to remain competitive and profitable.

However, as I will now show, the market often fails to deliver the optimal allocation of resources, resulting in economic inefficiency.

One reason market failure can occur is due to lack of competition. The existence of a monopoly (a single seller) may result in both productive and allocative inefficiency. Monopoly suppliers may exploit their market power by increasing price from P1 to P2 and restricting output to Q1, below the allocatively efficient level of output Q* where P = MC. This results in a deadweight loss to society of XYZ in fig. 3. They may also fail to minimise average cost due to lack of competition. To improve economic efficiency, the government could impose price controls or open the market up to competition through deregulation. This should result in lower prices and an increase in output towards the allocatively efficient level, Q*.

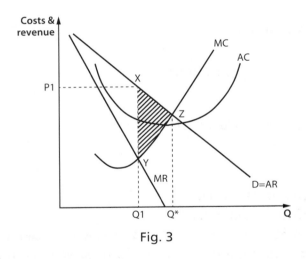

Fig. 3

However, in order to force the monopoly to operate at Q*, the government would require an accurate knowledge of the costs of the firm, which it is unlikely to have. Also, opening a monopoly up to competition may reduce dynamic efficiency as firms will have less profit to invest in research and development, which may prevent economic efficiency from being achieved in the longer run.

Another reason for market failure is the existence of externalities. Without government intervention, private firms motivated by profit may ignore the external costs of production, such as pollution. This may lead to too many resources being allocated to the production of goods with negative externalities such as oil and hence economic inefficiency. Through intervention, the government could correct for this by regulating firms and fining them for the damage they do to the environment as in the case of the Deepwater Horizon oil disaster. However, as external costs are difficult to estimate in monetary terms, the government may impose regulations and fines that are too harsh or too lenient, thereby failing to achieve economic efficiency.

The market may also fail to achieve an efficient allocation of resources due to information failure. Without government intervention, information failure may result in consumers purchasing too many demerit goods such as cigarettes and not enough merit goods such as vaccinations. Here, economic efficiency could be improved by government through direct provision of merit goods such as education. They could also correct for information failure by funding awareness campaigns that inform consumers of the harmful effects of demerit goods and the benefits of merit goods. Indirect taxes and subsidies could also be used to influence consumption of these goods and improve economic efficiency. Whether economic efficiency is achieved, however, will depend on the government correctly identifying which goods are merit goods and which are demerit goods and imposing laws and regulations appropriately.

In the absence of government intervention, there may also be missing markets for public goods such as street lighting and national defence due to the free-rider problem. A government could overcome this problem through direct provision of public goods using tax revenue. However, economic efficiency will only be improved if the government makes the right decisions about which goods to provide.

While it is theoretically possible for markets to achieve economic efficiency without government intervention, I believe that it is unlikely to happen due to the various forms of market failure. In my view therefore, it is only possible for economic efficiency to be achieved with some intervention from government. That said, I also believe that government intervention is more likely to 'improve' economic efficiency rather than actually 'achieve' it as governments are unlikely to have all the information they need to make the best decisions. Governments may also make decisions based on political self-interest, which is likely to worsen economic efficiency rather than achieve it.

Other areas for discussion:

- Positive externalities of consumption and/or production with diagrams.

- Immobility of factors of production (occupational and geographical immobility) leading to market failure.

- Other forms of government intervention such as pollution permits, maximum/minimum prices, etc.

AO2: Reference is made to the context of the exam question, i.e. the Deepwater Horizon oil spill.

AO4: Comment evaluating the effectiveness of government intervention in terms of the extent to which it affects output.

AO4: Comment evaluating the effectiveness of government policy in terms of the types of goods that are being regulated.

AO4: Explicit reference made to the wording of the question followed by a justified opinion.

- Corruption within some governments may lead to economic inefficiency.
- Conflicting objectives and excessive administrative costs may lead to 'government failure'.

LevelUP: Remember to provide a 'balanced' response to the question. For the question above, it would be easy to spend all of your time writing about the different types of market failures. However, this would leave the other parts of the question unanswered, severely limiting your overall mark. It's always best to manage your time so that you are able to produce a balanced response that addresses all parts of the question.

Self-reflection

Think about your overall response to this question and note down at least one:

- **what went well** (WWW) – something you did well in your response
- **even better if** (EBI) – something you could have done better

Keep these points in mind and use them to improve your next attempt at an essay question.

A-level
Economics

Practice paper for AQA

Paper 2

National and international economy

Time allowed: 2 hours

Materials

For this paper you must have:
- some paper or a notepad for your answers
- a calculator.

Instructions
- Use black ink or black ball-point pen. Pencil should only be used for drawing.
- In **Section A**, answer **EITHER** Context 1 **OR** Context 2.
- In **Section B**, answer **one** essay.

Information
- There are 80 marks available on this paper.
- The marks for questions are shown in brackets.

Name: ....

Paper 2 National and international economy
DATA RESPONSE QUESTIONS

Section A

Answer EITHER Context 1 OR Context 2

Context 1 (Total for this context: 40 marks)

Unemployment and Economic Growth

Study **Extracts A, B and C** and then answer all parts of **Context 1** that follow.

Extract A: Involuntary part-time employment

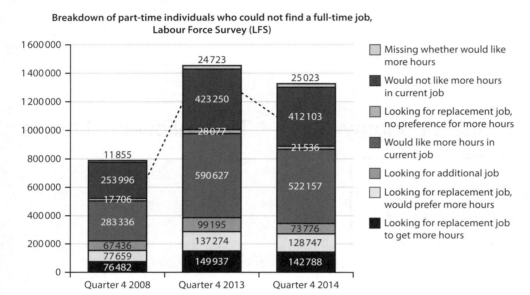

Extract B: Unemployment falls to lowest level in 11 years

The level of unemployment in any given country is a measure of economic health.

In the second quarter of 2016, the unemployment rate in the UK declined to 4.9%, the lowest figure since October 2005. There were 1.65 million unemployed people, 54,000 fewer than in the first quarter of 2016 and 201,000 fewer than for a year earlier.

5 The inactivity rate had also fallen. In the same quarter, there were 8.87 million people aged 16 to 64 who were economically inactive, 46,000 fewer than the first quarter of 2016 and 181,000 fewer than a year earlier. Thus, the inactivity rate was 21.6%, the lowest since comparable records began in 1971.

Commensurate with an unemployment rate at its lowest since 2008, the employment rate reached a record high of 74.4%. There were 31.70 million people in work, 176,000 more than the first quarter
10 of 2016 and 624,000 more than for a year earlier. 23.19 million were working full-time, 401,000 more than for a year earlier; 8.52 million were working part-time, 223,000 more than for a year earlier. As a result, the employment rate was 74.4%, the highest since comparable records began in 1971.

As a result of healthy employment figures, average weekly earnings for employees in the UK increased in nominal terms by 2.3% (including bonuses) and by 2.2% (excluding bonuses) compared
15 with a year earlier.

Extract C: UK GDP growth slumps to half previous rate

According to a respected independent thinktank, UK economic growth showed signs of struggle in the middle period of 2016.

Based on its estimates, the National Institute of Economic and Social Research (NIESR) calculated that gross domestic product (GDP) grew by 0.3% in the three months ending in July 2016, down from 6%
5 in the three months to June. This was short of consensus City forecasts for a 0.4% increase.

NIESR said the estimate was consistent with its latest quarterly forecast of a 0.2% contraction in the third quarter. This is worse than the market expected and adds credence to predictions that the economy will contract in the third quarter and then fall into recession. Indeed, the thinktank predicted an even-money chance of a technical recession between the third quarter of 2016 and the
10 final quarter of 2017.

Commentators observed that this was a marked economic slowdown: 'The month-on-month profile suggests that the third quarter has got off to a weak start, with output declining in July. Estimates suggest that there is around an evens chance of a technical recession by the end of 2017.'

The month-on-month profile suggests output declined in July by 0.2%, though NIESR stressed that
15 monthly calculations are volatile and cautioned against 'over-interpreting developments in the fundamentals of the economy from any single month'.

QUESTION 1

Using the data in **Extract A**, calculate to **two** decimal places the percentage change in the total number of individuals looking to increase the number of hours they work from 2008 to 2014.

[2 Marks]

QUESTION 2

Explain how the data in **Extract A** shows that measuring unemployment may be inaccurate.

[4 Marks]

QUESTION 3

Extract B (lines 2–3) states that the 'unemployment rate in the UK declined to 4.9%, the lowest figure since October 2005'.

With the help of a diagram, explain how low levels of unemployment may cause possible conflicts between macroeconomic policy objectives.

[9 Marks]

QUESTION 4

Extract C (lines 11–13) states 'The month-on-month profile suggests that the third quarter has got off to a weak start, with output declining in July. Estimates suggest that there is around an evens chance of a technical recession by the end of 2017'.

Using the data in the extracts and your economic knowledge, evaluate the view that low unemployment is the main reason for improved economic growth.

[25 Marks]

Context 2 (Total for this context: 40 marks)

Study **Extracts D, E and F** and then answer **all** parts of Context 2 that follow.

Extract D: UK Government spending

Fiscal years 2016–2018

Spending amounts in billions GBP

Year	2016 Spending		% of GDP	2017 Spending		% of GDP	2018 Spending		% of GDP
Pensions	154.7	a	8.25	156.9	e	8.07	158.6	e	7.85
Health care	138.7	e	7.4	142.7	g	7.34	146.4	g	7.25
Education	84.0	e	4.48	85.2	g	4.39	86.2	g	4.27
Defence	44.8	e	2.39	45.6	g	2.35	47.0	g	2.32
Welfare	112.9	e	6.02	113.1	g	5.82	111.6	g	5.52
Protection	29.9	e	1.59	29.4	g	1.51	30.5	g	1.51
Transport	26.3	e	1.4	28.3	g	1.45	29.4	g	1.45
General government	14.1	e	0.75	15.3	g	0.79	14.5	g	0.72
Other spending	17.1	e	0.91	18.6	g	0.96	18.3	g	0.91
Interest	45.7	e	2.44	48.5	g	2.5	51.7	g	2.56
Total spending	761.9	e	40.64	784.1	g	40.36	796.7	g	39.43
Public net debt	1590.6	a	84.84	1638.4	e	84.34	1676.9	e	82.99
Current budget deficit	39.0	e	2.08	19.1	e	0.98	3.5	e	0.17

a – actual outturn; *e* – estimate in HM Treasury 2016 Budget; *g* – 'guesstimated' projection by ukpublicspending.co.uk

Extract E: Real wages growth remains low for UK workers

The UK's record in real term wage drops is equalled only by Greece within the Organisation for Economic Co-operation and Development's (OECD) 35 member states. The financial crisis started a chain of events that has seen wages fall in real terms by 10.4% – and there has been little sign of recovery.

The fall is the biggest among leading OECD countries, including Portugal, Spain, France, Germany
5 and Ireland. The UK, Greece and Portugal were the only OECD countries where real wages, a measure which takes inflation into account, fell.

Trade Union Congress (TUC) General Secretary Frances O'Grady said: 'Wages fell off the cliff after the financial crisis and have barely begun to recover'. As the Bank of England recently argued, the majority of UK households have endured a 'lost decade of income'.

10 'People cannot afford another hit to their pay packets. Working people must not foot the bill for a downturn in the way they did for the bankers' crash.' This shows why the government needs to invest in large infrastructure projects to create more decent, well-paid jobs. 'Other countries have shown that it is possible to increase employment and living standards at the same time.'

A Treasury spokesman said: 'This analysis ignores the point that following the so-called "Great
15 Recession" the UK employment rate has grown more than any G7 country, living standards have

reached their highest level and wages continue to rise faster than prices – and will be helped by the new National Living Wage.'

Extract F: UK spends less on health than European neighbours

According to research, by 2020 the UK will be spending £43bn a year less on healthcare than its European counterparts.

The King's Fund, which carried out an analysis for The Guardian newspaper, pointed out that the UK spent 8.5% of its Gross Domestic Product (GDP) on healthcare in 2013, putting it 13th out of the 15
5 original members of the European Union (EU).

Politicians speaking on behalf of the Labour Party claimed that Britain was becoming the 'sick person of Europe', while the Liberal Democrats warned the National Health Service (NHS) would 'crash' if it did not get more funding.

Professor John Appleby, the King's Fund chief economist, wrote: 'Whatever the flaws of international
10 comparisons, it's clear that the UK is currently a relatively low spender on healthcare, with a prospect of sinking further down the international league tables.'

He said the UK's GDP was predicted to grow by about 15% between 2014–15 and 2020–2021, but NHS spending would increase by just 5.2% over the same period under current plans.

Spending the same on healthcare as the 15 original EU members would take a huge rise in the NHS
15 budget. 'If we were to close the gap solely by increasing NHS spending, by 2020–21 it would take an increase of 30% (£43bn) in real terms to match the EU-14's level of spend in 2013, taking total NHS spending to £185bn', Professor Appleby said.

Increased funding alone is not necessarily the answer though. Research carried out by Carol Propper, of Imperial College, London, has found that when there is more competition, the performance of
20 hospitals improves. Propper has said that she is concerned that this focus on financial issues has distracted from efforts to increase choice for patients.

QUESTION 5

Using the total spending figures from the data in **Extract D**, calculate to one decimal place the change in GDP over the period.

[2 Marks]

QUESTION 6

Explain how the data in **Extract D** shows why there may be concerns about future economic growth rates in the UK.

[4 Marks]

QUESTION 7

Extract E (lines 2–3) states 'The financial crisis started a chain of events that has seen wages fall in real terms by 10.4% – and there has been little sign of recovery'.

Explain the effect falling real wages may have on households in the UK **and** what the government can do to improve living standards.

[9 Marks]

QUESTION 8

Extract F (lines 3–5) states 'the UK spent 8.5% of its Gross Domestic Product (GDP) on healthcare in 2013, putting it 13th out of the 15 original members of the European Union (EU)'.

Using the data in the extracts and your economic knowledge, evaluate the view that spending on healthcare should take top priority for the UK government.

[25 Marks]

Paper 2 – Section B

Answer **one** essay from this section.

Each essay carries 40 marks.

EITHER

Essay 1

> The Bank of England's Monetary Policy Committee (MPC) sets monetary policy to meet the 2% inflation target, and in a way that helps to sustain growth and employment. At its meeting in August 2016, the MPC unanimously voted to reduce the bank rate of interest to 0.25%.

QUESTION 9

Using examples to illustrate your answer, explain some of the factors considered by the MPC when setting the 'bank rate' each month.

[15 Marks]

QUESTION 10

Assess the importance of monetary policy for achieving an improvement in the performance of the UK economy.

[25 Marks]

OR

Essay 2

> In recent years, the UK government has undertaken a range of supply-side measures including reductions in corporation tax, welfare reforms and the privatisation of Royal Mail, to improve the productivity and competitiveness of the UK economy.

QUESTION 11

Explain how supply-side improvements in the economy can originate from the private sector, independently of the government.

[15 Marks]

QUESTION 12

Assess the view that supply-side policies are more effective in achieving economic growth than demand-side policies.

[25 Marks]

OR

Essay 3

> The current account deficit reflects Britain's trade gap with the rest of the world and the shortfall between money paid out by the UK and money coming in. It stood at 6.9% of GDP in the first quarter of 2016, down only marginally from a record high of 7.2% in the fourth quarter of 2015.

QUESTION 13

Explain the factors that may have contributed to the large current account deficit experienced by the UK.

[15 Marks]

QUESTION 14

Evaluate the view that protectionism is never the best option for an economy.

[25 Marks]

Mark scheme for Paper 2 – Section A

Context 1

QUESTION 1

Using the data in **Extract A**, calculate to **two** decimal places the percentage change in the total number of individuals looking to increase the number of hours they work from 2008 to 2014.

[2 Marks]

Self-assessment

In order to gain two marks for this answer, you need to:	Achieved	Area for development
• calculate the answer correctly		
• express the answer as a %age (%)		
• round the answer to two decimal places		

Award yourself a mark

- Incorrect answer (0 marks)
- Correct answer but not expressed as a percentage and/or rounded to one decimal place (1 mark)
- Correct answer expressed as a percentage and rounded to two decimal places (2 marks)

Example response

The total number of individuals looking to increase the number of hours they work in 2008 was (283,336 + 67,436 + 77,659 + 76482) = **504,913**

The total number of individuals looking to increase the number of hours they work in 2014 was (522,157 + 73,776 + 128,747 + 142,788) = **867,468**

The percentage change is therefore:

$$\frac{867,468 - 504,913}{504,913} \times 100 = \frac{362,555}{504,913} \times 100 = 71.81\%$$

QUESTION 2

Explain how the data in **Extract A** shows that measuring unemployment may be inaccurate.

[4 Marks]

Self-assessment

In order to gain four marks for this question, you need to:	Achieved	Area for development
• Show accurate use of evidence/data (1 mark)		
• Use evidence to explain underemployment exists (1 mark)		
• Use evidence to explain how/why underemployment may cause measure of unemployment to be inaccurate (up to 2 marks)		

Award yourself a mark

Award yourself 1 mark for achieving each of the above criteria.

Example response

Extract A shows 522,157 individuals in 2014 who would like more hours in their current job (**1 mark**). This can be considered as underemployment, which refers to individuals who are employed, but not effectively used (**1 mark**). Because those individuals currently employed in part-time work do not meet the Labour Force Survey criteria, they are not included in the measure of unemployment (**1 mark**). With so many of these workers looking for more hours, they are still actively seeking work, but are 'masked' from unemployment measures, making the figures inaccurate (**1 mark**).

QUESTION 3

Extract B (lines 2–3) states that the 'unemployment rate in the UK declined to 4.9%, the lowest figure since October 2005'.

With the help of a diagram, explain how low levels of unemployment may cause possible conflicts between macroeconomic policy objectives.

[9 Marks]

Self-assessment

Self-assess your response using the grade descriptors and levels of response on pages 9 and 15–19.

Example response

Analyse the example response below and consider how each of the grade descriptors is achieved using the annotations in the right hand column to help you. Go back and review your answer after analysing this response.

Possible response

Low levels of unemployment are associated with a positive output gap in an economy. This is because with lower levels of unemployment, more households have higher disposable income and consumer expenditure rises ('...earnings increased...' Extract B, lines 13–14), increasing aggregate demand (AD).

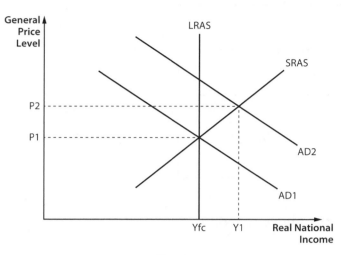

Fig. 1

As the graph shows, as AD rises from AD1 to AD2, national output increases from Yfc to Y1, causing an increase in the general price level from P1 to P2. The distance between Y1 and Yfc represents a positive output gap, where the current rate of growth is above the underlying trend rate of growth, i.e. actual output is above the full capacity level of the economy. During periods such as this there is increased demand-pull inflationary pressure, represented by the movement from P1 to P2. So whilst there are low levels of unemployment, this may lead to higher rates of inflation, making it more difficult for the government to achieve its 2% Consumer Price Index inflation target.

When AD is relatively high and economic growth is strong, confidence in the economy also rises, as would be expected with the employment rate at a record high (Extract B lines 11–12). This is associated with more spending and borrowing from households as there tends to be greater job security.

Higher consumer expenditure also puts pressure on the current account balance as incomes rise with economic growth. The net export component of AD, (X-M), may deteriorate with more spending on imported goods and services. This would cause a worsening of the existing current account deficit and would result in an imbalance in the balance of payments, contrary to the macroeconomic objective.

It is increasingly important for governments to ensure they use environmentally sustainable methods, and with low levels of unemployment and high rates of economic growth, this becomes difficult. Environmental conflicts are occurring in economies where rapid industrialisation is associated with the low unemployment and high growth, such as China. It is also evident in more densely populated areas of the UK, such as London, where concerns over air pollution have been described by MPs as a public health emergency.

Other areas for discussion:

- Negative impact on income distribution

- Rises in relative poverty

- Stable and sustained growth may be harder to maintain

- Depletion of non-renewable resources

LevelUP: Remember that you don't need to discuss **ALL** of these areas. These are just examples of other possible lines of analysis. It is much better to talk about one or two factors in detail than it is to list a large number of factors without developing any of them using chains of analysis. If you find yourself using lots of phrases that begin with 'and...', 'also...' and 'another...' then you may be listing and not analysing/evaluating.

Self-reflection

Think about your overall response to this question and note down at least one:

- **what went well** (WWW) – something you did well in your response

- **even better if** (EBI) – something you could have done better

Keep these points in mind and use them to improve your next attempt at an essay question.

QUESTION 4

Extract C (lines 11–13) states: 'The month-on-month profile, suggests that the third quarter has got off to a weak start, with output declining in July. Estimates suggest that there is around an evens chance of a technical recession by the end of 2017'.

Using the data in the extracts and your economic knowledge, evaluate the view that low unemployment is the main reason for improved economic growth.

[25 Marks]

Self-assessment

Self-assess your response using the grade descriptors and levels of response on pages 9 and 15–19.

Example response

Economic growth can best be defined as an increase in the productive capacity of the economy. This can be shown diagrammatically as an outward shift of the production possibility

> **AO1:** Shows understanding of economic growth and refers to diagram.

curve (PPC) or long-run aggregate supply curve (LRAS), shown as
LRAS1 to LRAS2 and Yfc1 to Yfc2 in fig. 1.

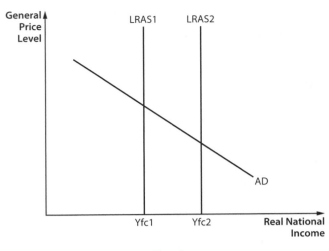

Fig. 1

Although raising national output using the existing capacity of
an economy is also referred to as economic growth (AD1 to AD2
and Y1 to Yfc in fig. 2), it is only achievable in the short run. 'True'
growth must be seen as improvements in productive potential, and
referred to as long-run growth.

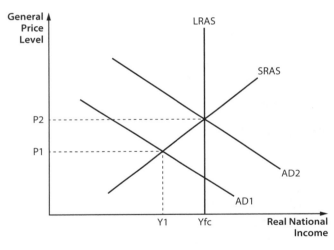

Fig. 2

There are many factors that can cause improved economic
growth, one of which is low unemployment. When
unemployment is low, employment levels are high and
households are earning more. With rising incomes come
associated increases in consumer spending and borrowing,
boosting AD and adding to growth. When there is an injection of
new demand into the circular flow, as with increased consumer
spending, there is likely to be a multiplier effect. This is because
an injection of higher income raises spending, thus creating more
income for recipients of the spending, and so on, further fuelling
economic growth.

AO1: Shows understanding
of link between low
unemployment, higher earnings
and economic growth.

AO3: Provides reasoning for an
expected multiplier effect.

The extent of this effect depends on households' marginal propensity to consume (MPC) and the level of withdrawals (savings, tax and imports) in the economy. When income is spent, it becomes someone else's income, so if their decision is to save more and spend less, the multiplier effect will be reduced and its effect on growth limited. For the UK, with a positive preference for imports, a large proportion of additional income is likely to be withdrawn from the circular flow as it is spent on imported goods and services. As such, higher spending as the result of low unemployment may not add to domestic growth as much as we might anticipate.

AO2: Good application to the UK context.

AO3: Explains reasoning for small multiplier.

AO4: Makes judgement based on reasoning from previous sentence.

Although earnings tend to grow with low unemployment, expenditure, and in particular larger purchases requiring borrowing, are often more closely related to consumer expectations and confidence. During times of uncertainty, such as those expressed for the UK in Extract C ('…estimates suggest that there is around an evens chance of a technical recession by the end of 2017', lines 12–13), households are more likely to defer borrowing and spending on items such as new cars or home renovations. In addition, with banks tightening lending requirements, households may find it more difficult to obtain loans for this type of spending. This may mean low unemployment without the expected boost to AD and growth.

AO2: Linking reasoning to extract reference.

AO4: Shows critical thinking of knowledge/theory/reasoning from previous paragraph.

AO4: Further develops reasoning for critical thinking presented and draws a conclusion.

Another driver of economic growth is investment by firms. Investment in new plant and equipment for example, increasing the scale of production of companies, raises the productive potential for an economy. Also, spending on research and development leads to improvements in technology and productivity, causing a shift in LRAS and improving productive capacity.

If AD is rising in the short run, without the associated improvements in the supply side of the economy as the result of increased investment, demand-pull inflation is the likely result, rather than improved growth. This causes higher rates of inflation by raising prices and thus reducing real incomes. So low unemployment without accompanied spending by firms may not improve, but rather hinder growth.

AO4: Draws a conclusion on alternate effect to analysis in previous paragraph.

Although low unemployment is an important reason for economic growth, it cannot be said to be the 'main' reason. Low unemployment alone is not sufficient, and needs to be accompanied by factors such as adequate investment expenditure, the availability of credit and a strong MPC for domestic goods and services. Without the combination of these, if an economy is to improve its economic growth, it is likely to be only in the short term and not sustainable in the long run.

AO4: Clear final judgement is made, supported by reasoning for conclusion.

Other areas for discussion:

- Use of monetary policy
- Governments' use of fiscal policy
- Reduction in protectionist measures
- Use of protectionism
- Supply-side policy measures
- Economic activity in other countries/globally
- Critical comments on what it means to 'improve' economic growth
- What is 'low' unemployment?

LevelUP: It is important to note the greater emphasis on analysis and evaluation in this response. Your answers to essay-style questions should always focus on these skills. Marks are scored for the quality of your analysis and evaluation, not for the amount of points you make. Just listing and briefly describing more points, without developing your arguments, will not score well.

Self-reflection

Think about your overall response to this question and note down at least one:

- **what went well** (WWW) – something you did well in your response
- **even better if** (EBI) – something you could have done better

Keep these points in mind and use them to improve your next attempt at an essay question.

Context 2

QUESTION 5

Using the total spending figures from the data in **Extract D**, calculate to **one** decimal place the change in GDP over the period.

[2 Marks]

Self-assessment

In order to gain two marks for this answer, you need to:	Achieved	Area for development
• calculate the answer correctly		
• express the answer as a %age (%)		
• round the answer to one decimal place		

Award yourself a mark

- Incorrect answer (0 marks)
- Correct answer but not expressed as a percentage and/or rounded to one decimal place (1 mark)
- Correct answer expressed as a percentage and rounded to one decimal place (2 marks)

Example response

Total spending in 2016: 761.9bn = **40.64% of GDP**

So: GDP in 2016 = $\dfrac{761.9}{0.4064}$ = **1874.75394bn**

Total spending in 2018: 796.7bn = **39.43% of GDP**

So: GDP in 2018 = $\dfrac{796.7}{0.3943}$ = **2020.54273bn**

%age change in GDP from 2016 to 2018

$$= \frac{2020.54273 - 1874.75394}{1874.7539} \times 100 = \textbf{7.8\%}$$

2 marks possible without workings (BUT, always show your workings!)

QUESTION 6

Explain how the data in **Extract D** show why there may be concerns about future economic growth rates in the UK.

[4 Marks]

Self-assessment

In order to gain four marks for this question, you need to:	Achieved	Area for development
• Show accurate use of evidence/data (1 mark)		
• Use evidence to explain future economic growth (1 mark)		
• Use evidence to explain why 'concerns' may be expressed about future growth (up to 2 marks)		

Award yourself a mark

Award yourself 1 mark for achieving each of the above criteria.

Example response

An important factor in economic growth is government spending, a significant component of aggregate demand (AD). Although Extract D predicted increases in total government spending from 761.9bn GBP to 796.7bn GBP over the period, this represents a fall from 40.6% to 39.4% as a percentage of GDP (**1 mark**), which may reduce future economic growth rates (**1 mark**). Another important feature of long-run economic growth is adequate healthcare provision. A healthy population means less working hours lost to illness, quicker recovery times and improved labour productivity. Extract D shows a fall in spending on healthcare as a percentage of GDP from 7.4% to 7.2% (**1 mark**), which may raise concerns about the economy's ability to maintain growth in the future (**1 mark**).

Another important factor for sustained long-term growth is adequate spending on education. The data shows a fall in education spending as a percentage of GDP from 4.5% to 4.3%. This too may be why there are concerns over future economic growth (**1 mark**).

QUESTION 7

Extract E (lines 2–3) states 'The financial crisis started a chain of events that has seen wages fall in real terms by 10.4% – and there has been little sign of recovery'.

Explain the effect falling real wages may have on households in the UK **and** what the government can do to improve living standards.

[9 marks]

Self-assessment

Self-assess your response using the grade descriptors and levels of response on pages 9 and 15–19.

Example response

Real wages are wages adjusted for changes in the price level over time. When real wages are falling, price increases are occurring faster than wages growth. With a fall in wages in real terms of 10.4% over the past decade (Extract E line 3), living standards will have fallen as increases in earnings will not have kept up with the rise in prices. This means a larger proportion of income will need to be devoted to spending to afford the same goods and services.

If households have 'endured a lost decade of income', as suggested (Extract E line 9), the government may look to undertake capital infrastructure schemes to create job opportunities and provide a stimulus to the economy. Because government spending is a component of aggregate demand (AD), spending on infrastructure projects such as new rail links will help raise economic growth $(Y1 - Y2)$. This provides a multiplier effect $(Y2 - Yfc)$ for the economy, increasing national income by more than the increase in spending, as shown in fig. 1.

AO1: Shows understanding of economic growth and refers to diagram.

AO2: Explicit use of extract material.

AO3: Provides reasoning for falling living standards.

AO1: Shows knowledge and understanding of appropriate government intervention.

AO3/AO2: Provides reasoning for expected impact on income in context of capital infrastructure improvements, i.e. rail links.

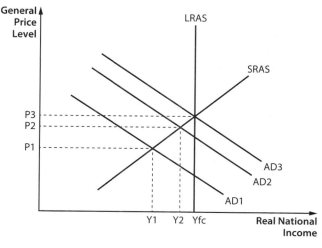

Fig. 1

The government could also reduce some taxes within the economy, such as corporation tax, to encourage more private sector investment. Firms investing more and expanding their operations would also provide more jobs throughout the economy, helping to maintain the standard of living for many workers.

Private sector investment would also have a positive multiplier effect, and often leads to improved technology and important productivity gains for the economy. This helps to maintain long-term growth, and subsequently, household incomes and living standards.

The government can also work to maintain a low inflation rate, and by doing so, help ensure wage growth is positive in real terms. There is a clear remit by the UK government for the Bank of England to achieve the 2.0% CPI inflation target. To keep inflation low, interest rates may rise, encouraging less spending and more saving, reducing demand-pull inflationary pressure in the economy. Higher interest rates can negatively impact on those households with debt, such as mortgages, as it will mean higher monthly repayments for those with a variable rate of interest.

AO1: Shows knowledge and understanding of appropriate government policy.

AO2: Good application to the UK context.

AO3: Develops reasoning as to how the policy would work to improve living standards.

Other areas for discussion:

- Reduced income tax

- Reduced VAT

- Raise tax-free threshold

- Increased spending on education

- Increased spending on welfare

- Welfare reform

- Increased support for new business start-ups

- Raise minimum wage

- Improve provision of public housing

Self-reflection

Think about your overall response to this question and note down at least one:

- **what went well** (WWW) – something you did well in your response
- **even better if** (EBI) – something you could have done better

Keep these points in mind and use them to improve your next attempt at an essay question.

QUESTION 8

Extract F (lines 3–5) states 'the UK spent 8.5% of its Gross Domestic Product (GDP) on healthcare in 2013, putting it 13th out of the 15 original members of the European Union'.

Using the data in the extracts and your economic knowledge, evaluate the view that spending on healthcare should take top priority for the UK government.

[25 Marks]

Self-assessment

Self-assess your response using the grade descriptors and levels of response on pages 9 and 15–19.

Example response

Spending on healthcare for the UK government is a top priority, and at an estimated 7.4% of GDP in 2016 it is the second largest area of spending. Only spending on pensions, at an estimated 8.25% of GDP (Extract D), is higher. This provides many benefits to the economy due to the positive externalities generated by a healthy population. A healthy population means a more productive labour force, with less time lost to illness and shorter recovery periods from medical treatment, aiding the economy's growth and competitiveness.

Although the UK government prioritises spending on healthcare in their budget, it could be seen as lacking when compared to that of its European neighbours. This is shown in Extract F with the UK described as a 'relatively low spender on healthcare' (line 10). If not given higher priority by the government, the UK may face difficulty in remaining competitive against other nations

AO1: Good use of extract data to support knowledge.

AO1: Shows knowledge and understanding of the macro-economic benefits of good healthcare provision.

in the future, as they make even greater productivity gains with a healthier workforce.

A healthy nation is necessary, but not sufficient, for the UK government to achieve its macroeconomic objectives. Therefore, spending on healthcare needs to be a top priority, but not the only one. In addition, an economy also needs a high standard of education for it to be competitive. Without both, the UK will find it difficult to compete with its trading partners. With spending on education to be reduced as a proportion of GDP by 2018 (Extract D), there is a strong argument for making education a higher priority.

AO3: Develops a chain of reasoning that spending on healthcare is important, but not sufficient.

The provision of healthcare in an economy cannot be measured by spending alone, however. What is more important is the quality of provision, rather than the amount spent. Creating a more competitive market for hospitals and healthcare providers in the UK may lead to a better quality of care and treatment. The principle of increased choice leading to improved medical treatment, as put forward by Carol Propper's research (Extract F lines 18–21) may improve quality without an associated spending increase.

AO4: Making a judgement on the importance of quality rather than spending shows evaluation.

AO2: Appropriate and explicit link to extract material.

Another extremely important priority for spending for the UK government to achieve its macroeconomic objectives is transportation. Efficient transportation infrastructure is needed for the economy to operate smoothly. An efficient public transportation network, for example, will improve the geographical mobility of labour, helping to lower unemployment. Additionally, with efficient and cost-effective public transportation, fewer individuals will use private transportation to travel to and from work. This would reduce the economy's carbon footprint and allow for environmentally sustainable growth in the future.

The difficulty in assessing the view that spending on healthcare should take top priority is that whilst it is important, it is not enough in itself. It can only take top priority if also supported by adequate spending and provision in other essential areas, such as education and transportation. It could be argued that perhaps the most important priority for any government needs to be ensuring that all objectives are pursued in a more environmentally sustainable way. If the world is unable to support our ongoing economic activity that will ultimately undermine the importance of any other single measure.

AO4: A clear final judgement is made and linked back to the question.

Other areas for discussion:

- Importance of trade

- Importance of communication

- Importance of welfare support for those in need

- Encouraging investment in research and development

- Energy provision

- Any other relevant area of government expenditure

Self-reflection

Think about your overall response to this question and note down at least one:

- **what went well** (WWW) – something you did well in your response

- **even better if** (EBI) – something you could have done better

Keep these points in mind and use them to improve your next attempt at an essay question.

Mark scheme for Paper 2 – Section B

Essay 1

The Bank of England's Monetary Policy Committee (MPC) sets monetary policy to meet the 2% inflation target, and in a way that helps to sustain growth and employment. At its meeting in August 2016, the MPC unanimously voted to reduce the bank rate of interest to 0.25%.

QUESTION 9

Using examples to illustrate your answer, explain some of the factors considered by the MPC when setting the 'bank rate' each month.

[15 Marks]

Self-assessment

Self-assess your response using the grade descriptors and levels of response on pages 9 and 15–19.

Example response

The bank rate is the official rate of interest at which the Bank of England lends to commercial banks. The objective of monetary policy is to influence economic activity in an attempt to maintain stable prices as defined by the government's inflation target of 2.0% as measured by CPI.

AO1: Clear understanding shown of bank rate and the objective of monetary policy.

The Monetary Policy Committee (MPC) analyses a wide range of economic data from both the demand side and supply side of the economy to assess inflationary pressure in the economy over a two year forecast horizon. For example, they consider GDP growth and spare capacity in the economy. Their main task is to set bank rates so that aggregate demand (AD) grows in line with productive potential, avoiding undue demand-pull pressures.

The MPC also take into account consumer and business confidence and expectations. When there is low consumer confidence, more households are likely to defer some spending decisions, and save rather than spend. So too with businesses. When expectations of future demand are poor, they are more likely to reduce their investment expenditure. Both of these will result in lower levels of AD and less inflationary pressure.

Another set of data the MPC use is equity markets (share prices) and house prices. These are both indicators of household wealth which influences borrowing and retail spending in the economy. When stock markets and/or housing markets are buoyant, a positive wealth effect for households encourages higher consumer spending, adding to demand-side inflationary pressure, as shown in fig. 1.

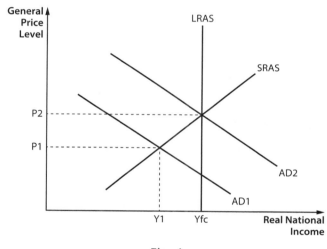

Fig. 1

The MPC also analyses wage growth data as a potential contributor to cost-push inflationary pressure. When wage growth is subdued and unit labour costs remain low, cost-push pressures to firms remain relatively weak. This reduces the need for firms to raise their prices in order to cover labour costs and maintain profit margins.

Information from outside the UK domestic economy is also important for the MPC to consider when setting the 'bank rate'. This includes trends in global exchange rate markets. A weakening currency will be a threat to inflation as it raises the price of imported goods and services. Other international markets analysed by the MPC include resources such as oil and copper. As these are both important resources in the production process for many firms, changes in global prices can have an impact on costs of production, and subsequently cost-push pressures in the UK economy.

AO2: Reference to specific commodity markets relevant to the UK.

Other areas for discussion:

- Unemployment figures
- Bank lending and household credit information
- International data including growth rates in other countries and regions, e.g. US, EU
- Policy stance of main trading partners
- Current account of balance of payments
- UK government fiscal stance

LevelUP: Diagrams need to be sufficiently large for the examiner to easily see what you have shown. A good rule of thumb is they should be about the size of your fist. They should also be neat and clearly labelled.

Self-reflection

Think about your overall response to this question and note down at least one:

- **what went well** (WWW) – something you did well in your response
- **even better if** (EBI) – something you could have done better

Keep these points in mind and use them to improve your next attempt at an essay question.

QUESTION 10

Assess the importance of monetary policy for achieving an improvement in the performance of the UK economy.

[25 Marks]

Self-assessment

Self-assess your response using the grade descriptors and levels of response on pages 9 and 15–19.

Example response

Monetary policy is a demand-side policy and involves the use of interest rates, money supply and exchange rates to manage the level of aggregate demand (AD). The objective is to achieve price stability (2% inflation target), and support the government's economic policies, including those for growth and employment. It is conducted by the MPC at the Bank of England and they have independent control over policy decisions. The main policy instrument has historically been interest rates, though this has

AO1: Shows good knowledge and understanding of monetary policy in the UK.

been accompanied by changes in the money supply through the use of quantitative easing in recent years.

There are several key indicators of economic performance, including:

- economic growth,
- unemployment,
- inflation,
- current account balance.

Monetary policy can be used to stimulate economic growth by raising aggregate demand (AD) within the economy. A reduction in interest rates is likely to encourage more investment spending by firms as it reduces the cost of borrowing, an important source of investment funds. With lower borrowing costs, firms are more likely to undertake investment decisions as they will see a greater return on their spending. This has the effect of boosting AD and creating jobs. It will also provide a positive multiplier effect, increasing national income by more than the injection of investment, see fig. 1.

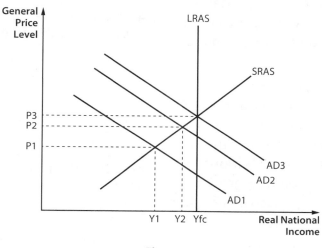

Fig. 1

Investment may not be as interest rate sensitive as expected though. The Keynesian view suggests firms' decisions may be influenced to a greater extent by 'animal spirits', i.e. confidence and expectations. If interest rates are lowered and the outlook for growth in the economy is weak, firms are less likely to borrow and spend on investment. Conversely, if firms' expectations for future growth are strong, higher interest rates may not deter their borrowing. Instead, they may look to recover additional costs from borrowing by raising prices in the future.

Monetary policy can also improve economic performance via the exchange rate. A reduction in interest rates is likely to be followed by a depreciation of the exchange rate. This is due largely to hot-money outflows, where available funds are withdrawn from domestic accounts and deposited abroad to earn higher returns.

A weaker currency will aid export industries as their goods and services become more price competitive in international markets. This can provide an additional boost to export earnings and allow for a period of export-led growth. This can be important for job creation in the export sector, and at the same time, help to reduce the current account deficit.

The gradualist approach to interest rate changes employed by the MPC however, mean that when interest rates are lowered it is likely to be by a small margin, often by only 0.25%. As such, any subsequent fall in the exchange rate may not be significant enough to provide a competitive edge for exporters, or any real stimulus to AD. Also, the effect of an exchange rate depreciation on export earnings is dependent on the price elasticity of demand for the UK's exports, and will cause a fall in revenue if demand for exports is price inelastic.

> **AO2/AO4:** The UK's use of interest changes considered critically in the context of a gradualist approach and reasons why this may not have the expected 'theoretical' effect.

With UK interest rates remaining so low for so long, the MPC have also introduced a programme of quantitative easing (QE) to introduce new liquidity into the economy. This is designed to encourage further lending by financial institutions, keep interest rates low and add a stimulus to the economy. The same policy has also been used in the US and the EU, though uncertainty remains over its use and effectiveness.

> **AO2:** Uses knowledge to apply to UK, EU and US context.

The greatest concern is that pumping new money into the economy will lead to higher inflation. Whilst inflation rates in the UK remain very low, some upward pressure on prices can perhaps be seen as a good thing. However, there are concerns that the longer term effect is likely to be too much inflation. Additionally, it may be argued that rather than stimulating economic growth, the additional money supply from QE has merely raised asset prices such as shares and housing.

> **AO4:** Questions the effectiveness of QE.

Although important for improving economic performance, monetary policy alone is not sufficient. It does not work in isolation, and must be supported by the use of fiscal policy and effective supply-side measures to improve economic performance. This allows sufficient growth in productive potential of the economy to accommodate the rising AD. Without adequate supply-side improvements, use of demand management through the implementation of monetary policy will more likely result in relatively short-term gains, and is unlikely to allow for continued improvements in long-run performance.

> **AO4:** Clear final judgement is made and linked back to the question.

Other areas for discussion:

• Provides price stability

• Protects living standards by maintaining real incomes

LevelUP: Try and keep your sentences relatively short and concise. It is better to avoid linking too many points together with commas. Instead, use a full stop and start a new sentence. This will help readability and will force you to structure your paragraphs using clear, logical chains of reasoning.

Self-reflection

Think about your overall response to this question and note down at least one:

- **what went well** (WWW) – something you did well in your response

- **even better if** (EBI) – something you could have done better

Keep these points in mind and use them to improve your next attempt at an essay question.

Essay 2

In recent years, the UK government have undertaken a range of supply-side measures including reductions in corporation tax, welfare reforms and the privatisation of Royal Mail, to improve the productivity and competitiveness of the UK economy.

Question 11

Explain how supply-side improvements in the economy can originate from the private sector, independently of the government.

[15 Marks]

Self-assessment

Self-assess your response using the grade descriptors and levels of response on pages 9 and 15–19.

Example response

Supply-side improvements refer to a range of measures and actions that result in the more efficient operation of markets and industries, and contribute to a faster underlying rate of growth of real national output. This is represented diagrammatically by an outward shift of the long-run aggregate supply (LRAS) curve, showing an increase in the productive potential of the economy, see fig. 1.

> **AO1:** Good knowledge and understanding shown of supply-side improvements (including diagrammatically).

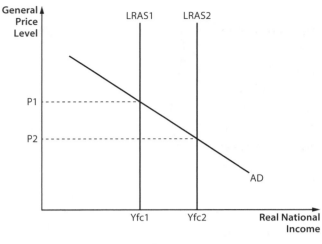

Fig. 1

Firms improving their provision of training for staff will help raise labour productivity, and thus aid supply-side improvements in the economy. For some firms this may simply involve providing training for their workers. For most though, improving training is more likely to mean raising the standard of training provided. This might mean using external providers to come and share best practice with workers, or sending workers to undertake off-the-job training provided by specialists, or a combination of both.

> **AO1:** Shows knowledge and understanding, applied to context.
>
> **AO3:** Develops a chain of reasoning to support the opening sentences of the paragraph.

Investing further in research and development will lead to a faster pace of innovation and invention. This should provide positive spill-over effects for the wider industry and economy as a whole. Increased competition in global markets, particularly in areas such as computing and mobile technology, has meant that firms are spending more on developing their technologies to remain competitive. This has led to improved communication abilities that have resulted in more efficient operations, and thus improved the supply-side performance of the economy.

> **AO2:** Good application to computing and mobile technology markets.

Similarly, increased competition arising from increasingly globalised markets has put pressure on firms to continually update and improve the capital they use in their production process. In car manufacturing for example, maintaining a competitive edge requires staying at the forefront of technological advances and investing heavily in appropriate machinery. This raises both capital and labour productivity in the industry and adds to supply-side improvements for the economy.

> **AO3:** Develops a chain of reasoning showing how supply-side improvements originate from the private sector.

Labour productivity may be improved by private sector employers providing their workforce with incentives such as productivity bonuses. To encourage improved output and efficiency from their workers, employers may offer monetary rewards for workers that can hit certain targets and thus raise their productivity. Incentives such as this can encourage workers to become more efficient by adopting better working practices in an attempt to meet the targets and earn higher income.

Other areas for discussion:

- FDI resulting in shared best practice and new technology for developing economies
- Improved labour market flexibility through increased use of zero-hour contracts
- Better technology allows for improved information provision of job vacancies and promotion opportunities

LevelUP: To help you frame your answer, try to use the wording of the question. Notice, for example, that this has been done to good effect in the last lines of the third and fourth paragraphs. Linking to the question in such an obvious way keeps you on track and signals your focus to the examiner.

Self-reflection

Think about your overall response to this question and note down at least one:

- **what went well** (WWW) – something you did well in your response
- **even better if** (EBI) – something you could have done better

Keep these points in mind and use them to improve your next attempt at an essay question.

QUESTION 12

Assess the view that supply-side policies are more effective in achieving economic growth than demand-side policies.

[25 Marks]

Self-assessment

Self-assess your response using the grade descriptors and levels of response on pages 9 and 15–19.

Example response

Supply-side policies are defined as a range of measures aimed at increasing long-run productive potential in the economy, through improving efficiency, productivity and competitiveness in the economy. The effect is shown by an outward shift of long-run aggregate supply (LRAS). Demand-side policies are targeted at managing the level of aggregate demand (AD) in the economy and are shown as outward movements of the AD curve. Economic growth can arise through increasing national output through the use of existing productive capacity, i.e. short-run growth, or through increasing productive capacity, i.e. long-run growth.

AO1: Good knowledge and understanding of both supply-side and demand-side policies.

Demand-side policies are more likely to result in short-run growth, but without necessarily increasing the capacity of the economy. Expansionary fiscal policy, for example lowering income tax for middle income earners, will lead to higher disposable income for many in the economy. With more income, consumer expenditure will rise, boosting AD. This will raise real GDP, increasing short-run economic growth, shown as the movement from AD1 to AD2 and Y1 to Y2, see fig. 1.

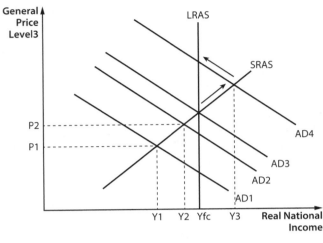

Fig. 1

However, the closer the economy is to operating at full capacity when fiscal policy is loosened, the less likely the rise in national output. This is because when there is little or no spare capacity, any further rises in AD will be transferred to the price level, having an inflationary effect. As demand rises, if firms do not have the capacity to meet that demand, they are more likely to increase prices. This can be shown as the movement from AD3 to AD4, with no rise in real national output in the longer term.

AO3: Develops reasoning for inflationary effect when economy is operating at full capacity.

Similarly, expansionary monetary policy can act to stimulate AD, causing higher real national output, i.e. short-run economic growth, by lowering interest rates. As seen in recent years though, interest rates have already been extremely low, and many firms have been operating in the UK with large spare capacity. The recent drop from 0.5% to 0.25% of the bank rate by the MPC gives little additional incentive to borrow. This coupled with spare capacity, doesn't encourage firms to invest. Monetary policy would be ineffective at encouraging higher rates of economic growth.

AO2: Good use of knowledge re: recent UK developments.

Supply-side policies are more likely to result in long-run economic growth, due to their impact on efficiency, productivity and competitiveness. Measures such as the sale of state monopolies to encourage more competition, place competitive pressures on firms in the market. Also, strengthening powers of regulatory bodies such as the Competition and Markets Authority (CMA) improves competition and helps avoid anti-competitive practices such as price fixing and bid-rigging. Increased competition forces firms to continually strive to make productivity and efficiency gains. These gains lead to an improvement in productive potential for the economy and shift LRAS to the right, see fig. 2.

AO3: Develops a good chain of reasoning to show the expected effect of improved competition through the sale of state monopolies.

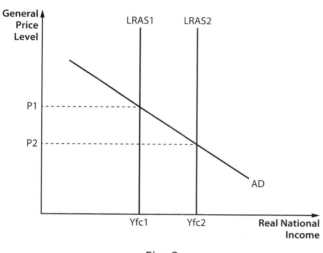

Fig. 2

For many economies however, this process has already been undertaken by the government, e.g. the UK's sale of Royal Mail. There are very few public sector monopolies left in place, so there is little scope for this type of measure. Additionally, the sale of state-run monopolies does not guarantee more competitive markets. It may simply result in the transfer of ownership from public to private. This moves monopoly power into the hands of private firms with a need to satisfy their stakeholders. As such, choice may be reduced and prices may rise, resulting in reduced consumer welfare and hindering growth.

AO2: Good application to the UK context.

AO4: Critical reasoning explaining why 'theoretical', expected effect may not occur.

In conclusion, to achieve economic growth both supply and demand-side policies need to work together, as neither is sufficient alone. Stimulating AD is only effective in the short term, and requires improvements in productive capacity to avoid undue inflation. Also, strengthening the supply side of the economy is needed to provide an efficient, productive and competitive platform for economic growth in the longer term.

AO4: Clear, final judgement made with supporting reasoning.

Other areas for discussion:

• Reduced interest rates to encourage investment

• Reduced interest rates to increase household spending

Self-reflection

Think about your overall response to this question and note down at least one:

- **what went well** (WWW) – something you did well in your response
- **even better if** (EBI) – something you could have done better

Keep these points in mind and use them to improve your next attempt at an essay question.

QUESTION 13

Essay 3

The current account deficit reflects Britain's trade gap with the rest of the world and the shortfall between money paid out by the UK and money coming in. It stood at 6.9% of GDP in the first quarter of 2016, down only marginally from a record high of 7.2% in the fourth quarter of 2015.

Explain the factors that may have contributed to the large current account deficit experienced by the UK.

[15 Marks]

Self-assessment

Self-assess your response using the grade descriptors and levels of response on pages 9 and 15–19.

Example response

The balance of payments is a record of all financial transactions between one economy and the rest of the world. It is broken into three accounts: current account, capital account and financial account. The current account records the balance of trade in goods, balance of trade in services, primary income flows and secondary income flows. For a current account deficit, the net outflows for these four categories are greater than the net inflows.

AO1: Shows clear understanding of balance of payments, current account components and deficit.

One reason the UK may have a large deficit on current account is a trade deficit, i.e. if the UK spends more on goods and services than it earns from exports. The UK has a deficit of trade in goods, or visible trade, which includes oil and other energy products, finished manufactured goods, foodstuffs, raw materials and components.

The manufacturing sector has been in decline in the UK for many years as it has faced increased competition from emerging economies able to produce at much lower costs. As such there is now an imbalance in the export and imports of goods, such as motor vehicles and consumer electronic products. Although the UK has a strong base in the trade of services, particularly banking and finance, the surplus of trade in services is not large enough to compensate for the large deficit on trade in goods.

AO1/AO2: Identifies cause and links to UK context.

AO3/AO2: Develops reasoning for the UK's trade in goods deficit despite surplus of trade in services.

A relatively strong currency can contribute to a large value of imports. With the pound relatively strong against many trading partners' currencies, imported goods and services are relatively cheap for UK consumers. This encourages them to purchase foreign produced imports, rather than the more expensive domestically produced goods. A strong currency also makes travelling abroad more appealing, making it more likely that there will be greater outflows of money for the purpose of tourism.

AO3: Develops chain of reasoning relating to strong currency as a cause.

Rising real incomes in the UK can lead to increased spending by households, and falling unemployment can add to consumer confidence. This raises consumption throughout the economy. With a positive preference for imports, much of that spending will be directed toward imported goods and services. Also, when demand for imports is relatively income elastic, any increase in incomes will be accompanied by rapid increases in spending on imports.

AO1: Identifies relevant cause.

AO3: Develops chain of reasoning from opening sentence.

Other areas for discussion:

- UK firms outsourcing materials and component parts
- Off-shoring to access cheaper labour from emerging markets

LevelUP: When planning your response, 'play to your strengths'. Don't avoid topics that you find difficult, but don't worry about being perfect in these areas. The danger is that you get tied up trying to explain something you have weak understanding of. Try to reference the more difficult theory/topic ('...X would also be significant...') but quickly move on to areas where you are stronger and can develop stronger logical chains of reasoning.

Self-reflection

Think about your overall response to this question and note down at least one:

- **what went well** (WWW) – something you did well in your response

- **even better if** (EBI) – something you could have done better

Keep these points in mind and use them to improve your next attempt at an essay question.

QUESTION 14

Evaluate the view that protectionism is never the best option for an economy.

[25 Marks]

Self-assessment

Self-assess your response using the grade descriptors and levels of response on pages 9 and 15–19.

Example response

Protectionism refers to any attempt to impose restrictions on trade in goods and services, and the aim is usually to provide domestic firms some degree of 'protection' from international competition.

> **AO1:** Good knowledge/ definition of protectionism. Remember, starting with a definition is a good tactic.

The dominant thinking in economic theory today certainly leans toward free trade because it should result in mutual welfare gains between trading partners. It should also result in a more competitive environment for firms, leading to efficiency gains and a faster pace of innovation and invention. Greater exploitation of scale economies occurs, lowering prices and providing jobs. Although there are many strong arguments for free trade, there are still reasons why countries may quite rightly choose to employ some protectionist measures.

The use of tariffs, a tax on imports, raises the domestic price of foreign produced goods and services. When imposed appropriately, tariffs can help reduce negative externalities, protect employment and provide additional welfare gains to domestic producers.

> **AO1:** Shows clear understanding of tariffs and their effect.

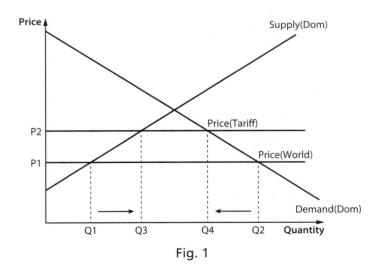

Fig. 1

After the tariff is imposed, the volume of imports will be reduced from Q1Q2 to Q3Q4. In Malaysia, for example, the government imposes a 'sin tax' on alcohol imports to reduce negative externalities associated with drinking, as they feel alcohol consumption is contrary to their moral and religious beliefs. As such, protecting their consumers from the easy availability of cheap alcohol can be seen to be in their national interest. Some may view this policy to be limited however, due to its regressive effects. It may also be considered discriminatory against those who live in Malaysia but do not hold the same religious and moral views as the government.

AO1: Makes appropriate use of tariff diagram.

AO2: Application of tariff use to Malaysia.

AO3: Develops chain of reasoning for Malaysian taxation.

AO4: Provides critical view of tariff used in this example.

The imposition of tariffs should also be considered when applied to infant industries, i.e. those where domestic producers are yet to have grown sufficiently to compete against multinationals, for example. Without some form of protection from well-established international competitors that have already developed large scale economies and operate at lower unit costs, infant industries may never make it off the ground.

This is particularly relevant to firms operating in less developed economies that have only recently gained access to necessary capital and technology. Although contrary to the arguments for free trade, this form of protectionism may hold greater strength when considered in terms of global equity. Surely it is only fair to take back some of the existing advantage held by well-established firms, giving young entrepreneurs a chance to compete?

AO2/AO4: Applies thinking to developing economies and expresses view on relevance/importance.

AO4: Makes a clear judgement for justification of tariffs when considered from an alternate perspective.

Protectionism may also be beneficial when employed strategically to protect domestic employment, investment and subsequently consumption. Governments may identify 'goods of strategic importance', such as energy, defence or even certain foodstuffs. This was the case with France and Danone, and the protection provided to avoid unwanted foreign takeovers. Such actions may help to ensure an economy doesn't suffer from large-scale unemployment, or reliance on others for the basic provision of essential items.

AO1: Shows clear understanding of valid argument for protectionism.

AO2: Good application to real world context.

AO3: Provides conclusive chain of reasoning.

To conclude, protectionism is not always a second-best option, it is in some cases the only option. The merits of free trade are perhaps questionable when assessed against income and wealth inequality, and certain cases of economic nationalism. For the global economy to be strong, individual domestic economies need to be strong. Some nations are weaker than others, and until they can carry their own weight, protectionism is indeed the best option for their governments.

AO4: Provides clear final judgement with supporting justification.

Other areas for discussion:

- Improvement of balance of payments
- Anti-dumping arguments
- Other market failure arguments
- Differences in absolute and comparative advantage between countries

LevelUP: A useful way to structure your answers is: 'one paragraph, one point'. That is, every paragraph should have one clear focus and follow the 'PEEEL' approach (Point – Example – Explain – Evaluate – Link). Consider, for example, the paragraph following fig. 1 – it starts with knowledge (AO1), is supported by real-world application (AO2), develops reasoning (AO3), and then offers an evaluative comment (AO4).

However, if your chain of reasoning requires a longer response, it is sometimes better to split this over two paragraphs. The approach here would be to present your analysis in the first paragraph and your evaluation in the second.

Self-reflection

Think about your overall response to this question and note down at least one:

- **what went well** (WWW) – something you did well in your response
- **even better if** (EBI) – something you could have done better

Keep these points in mind and use them to improve your next attempt at an essay question.

A-level
Economics
Practice paper for AQA

Paper 3

Economic principles and issues

Time allowed: 2 hours

Materials

For this paper you must have:
- some paper or a notepad for your answers
- a calculator.

Instructions
- Answer **all** questions.
- Use black ball-point pen. Do **not** use pencil.
- You will need to refer to the source booklet provided to answer **Section B**.
- For **Section A**, fill in the answer lozenges, as instructed, on the paper.
- For **Section B**, write your answer on the paper or notepad.
- Do all rough work on the paper or notepad.

Information
- The marks for questions are shown in brackets.
- The maximum mark for this paper is 80.
- No deductions will be made for wrong answers.

Name: ....

Paper 3 Economic principles and issues

Section A

Answer **all** questions in this section

Only **one** answer per question is allowed.

For each answer completely fill in the lozenge alongside the appropriate answer.

CORRECT METHOD [●]   WRONG METHODS [⊗] [⊙] [⊜] [✓]

If you want to change your answer you must cross out your original answer as shown. [⊗]

If you wish to return to an answer previously crossed out, ring the answer you now wish to select. [⊗]

0 1   Which one of the following is a true statement about the relationship between marginal costs and average costs?

A   When marginal costs are low, average costs are low

B   When average costs are at their minimum, marginal costs are falling

C   When marginal costs are below average costs, average costs are falling

D   When marginal costs are high, average costs are high

0 2   Which one of the following would be classified as a supply-side policy measure?

A   An increase in interest rates

B   A reduction in the government's fiscal deficit

C   New legal controls designed to restrict the power of trade unions

D   The imposition of tariffs on imported goods

0 3 The relative prices of goods reflect their marginal utilities rather than their total utilities.

Which of the following is explained by this statement?

A   The rationing function of prices

B   The law of diminishing returns

C   A limitation of marginal utility theory

D   The paradox of value

0 4 A firm currently has a labour force of 50 workers and its total wage bill is $20,000 per day. If the number of workers employed increases to 51, the firm's daily wage bill would increase by $602.

What is the marginal cost of labour per day?

A $2

B $602

C $1002

D $20,002

0 5 Country A is operating a floating exchange rate and experiences a depreciation of its currency. As a result, its export revenue declines.

Which of the following statements could explain this?

A   Demand for Country A's exports is price elastic

B   Country A's government is operating a budget deficit

C   The price elasticity of supply of Country A's exports is greater than 1

D   The price elasticity of demand of Country A's exports lies between 0 and −1

0 6 The diagram below shows the market supply and demand curves for instant noodles.

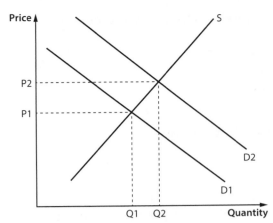

Assuming that instant noodles are an inferior good, the change in demand and equilibrium price shown can be explained by:

A A fall in households' disposable income

B The introduction of a value added tax (VAT) exemption on instant noodles

C A fall in the cost of packaging for instant noodles

D The removal of a subsidy previously paid to instant noodle producers

0 7 The Lorenz curve is used to measure which of the following?

A The level of poverty in developing economies

B The level of welfare in developing economies

C Inequality of income distribution

D The size of the investment accelerator

0 8 A specific tax is placed on each bottle of wine sold. In the diagram, S1 is the supply curve before the imposition of the tax and S2 the supply curve after the imposition of the tax.

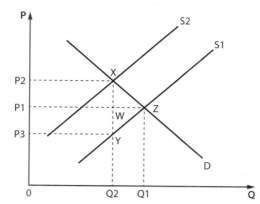

Which area represents the revenue received by the government from the tax?

A P2XWP1

B P2XQ20

C P1WYP3

D P2XYP3

0 9 Under the assumption of *ceteris paribus*, which of the following would cause an outward shift in the short-run aggregate supply curve of an economy?

A An appreciation of the domestic currency

B An increase in the money supply

C A reduction in interest rates

D A reduction in income tax rates

1 0 In an attempt to reduce carbon emissions, a government has introduced a new policy requiring energy companies to use cleaner methods of production. This has caused an increase in the operating costs for those companies affected.

What effect will this have on the private, external and social costs of production in the affected industries?

	Private cost	External cost	Social cost
A	Increase	Decrease	Decrease
B	Increase	Decrease	Uncertain
C	Decrease	Increase	Uncertain
D	Decrease	Increase	Decrease

1 1 In 2009 the US Central Bank, the Federal Reserve, undertook quantitative easing through the purchase of securities in the open market.

What policy use describes this action?

A Reflationary fiscal policy

B Deflationary fiscal policy

C Expansionary monetary policy

D Supply-side policy

1 2 Country A has a comparative advantage in the production of rice and Country B has a comparative advantage in the production of mobile phones. Which of the following would explain why they choose not to specialise and trade with each other?

A Trade is based on absolute rather than comparative advantage

B The transport costs are low in relation to the difference in opportunity costs between the countries

C Global demand for both rice and mobile phones is rising

D The exchange rate lies outside the opportunity cost ratios of the countries

1 3 Country A only trades with two other countries, the UK and France. 80% of Country A's trade is with the UK and 20% is with France. If the original value of the trade-weighted index is 100, what will be the new value of the trade-weighted index if Country A experiences a 20% increase in its currency value against Sterling and a 40% increase in its currency value against the Euro?

A   114

B   120

C   124

D   160

1 4 The diagram below shows the quantity produced of a good (Q1) as a result of market forces.

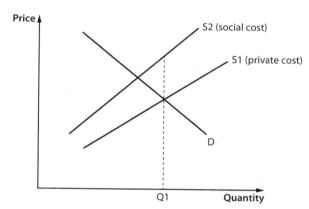

What is most likely to have led to this level of output?

A   An efficient allocation of resources

B   An absence of property rights

C   The imposition of an indirect tax

D   Price instability

1 5 The long-run trend rate of growth for the UK economy has been approximately 2.5% since 1960. As a result of the financial crisis of 2008–09, economic growth for the UK economy fell to approximately 0.6% in 2010.

Which of the following diagrams best represents what the UK economy experienced in 2010?

A

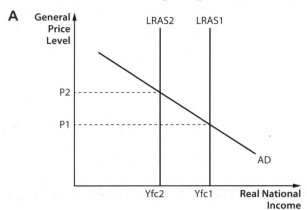

B

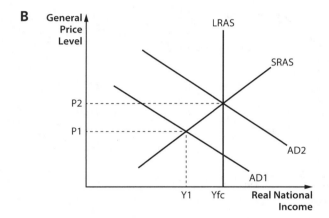

C

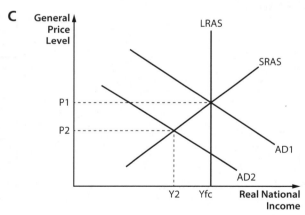

D

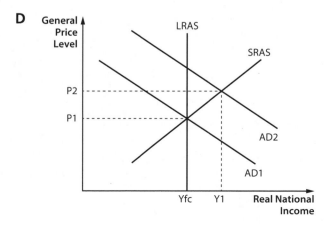

1 6 The cross price elasticity of demand for coffee with respect to tea is +2.0. If the price of tea falls by 10%, the demand for coffee will:

A increase by 10%

B increase by 20%

C decrease by 10%

D decrease by 20%

1 7 The diagram below shows the relationship between the inflation rate and the unemployment rate.

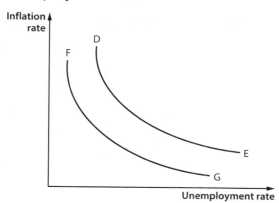

What would cause the curve DE to shift to FG?

A The expectation of a fall in inflation

B An increase in government spending

C A reduction in wages growth

D An increase in interest rates

1 8 The diagram below shows an individual worker's supply of labour curve.

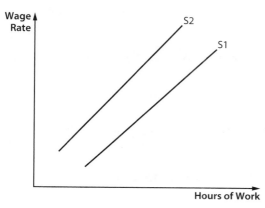

What could cause the curve to shift from S1 to S2?

A A fall in wages

B The removal of an indirect tax

C An increase in the opportunity cost of leisure

D An increased preference for leisure

1 9 A closed economy with no government has a marginal propensity to consume of 0.8. The full employment level of national income is $80,000m. The current level of national income is $50,000m.

By how much must investment increase if the economy is to reach its full employment level of national income?

A $3000m

B $6000m

C $8000m

D $30,000m

2 0 A country experiences a fall in its annual inflation rate from 7% to 4% over the period of a year.

Which statement is correct?

A There has been an increase in the cost of living

B Living standards have improved

C The price level has fallen

D There has been a decrease in the Consumer Price Index

2 1 A regressive tax system is one in which:

A the proportion of income paid in tax is the same for all individuals

B low income earners pay more in taxes than high income earners

C high income earners pay a lower proportion of their income in taxes than low income earners

D high income earners pay a greater proportion of their income in taxes than low income earners

2 2 Which statement about externalities is correct?

A Externalities are considered by private firms when making price and output decisions

B Externalities always lead to an over provision of a good or service by the market

C Externalities are easier to value in money terms than private costs and benefits

D Externalities can be both harmful and beneficial

2 3 A 6% increase in the money supply leads to a 10% increase in the nominal value of a country's income. According to the monetarist theory, what can be assumed from this?

A The inflation rate has increased by 4%

B There has been an increase in marginal income tax rates

C There has been an increase in interest rates

D There has been an increase in the velocity of circulation of money

2 4 The diagram below shows the marginal product of labour (MPL) curve for a firm.

Labour is considered a variable factor whilst all other factors of production are fixed.

Which of the following statements is correct for the level of employment OX?

A The firm is minimising its marginal cost of production

B The firm is maximising its output

C The firm is minimising the number of workers employed

D The firm is making a loss

2 5 An economy is operating at a point inside its production possibility boundary.

Why would this be described as inefficient?

A   Individuals are enjoying too much leisure and not working hard enough   ⬭

B   Labour and capital are combined in the wrong proportions   ⬭

C   More of one good or service can be produced without decreasing production of another   ⬭

D   There are shortages of some goods and services and surpluses of others   ⬭

2 6 A profit maximising firm operates in a perfectly competitive market. It is currently producing at a level of output where its marginal cost is above its average cost but below the market price.

What will be the likely effect on output and price in the short run?

A   Increased output and decreased price   ⬭

B   Increased output and no change to price   ⬭

C   Decreased output and increased price   ⬭

D   Decreased output and no change to price   ⬭

2 7 Real GNP per capita may be considered unreliable as an indicator when comparing the standard of living between different countries.

What adjustments could be made to improve its usefulness when making comparisons between countries?

A   Adjusting to allow for different population sizes between countries   ⬭

B   Adjusting to allow for different rates of inflation between countries   ⬭

C   Adjusting to allow for differences in the hidden economies between countries   ⬭

D   Using market exchange rates instead of purchasing power parity exchange rates   ⬭

2 8 Which of the following is likely to increase a country's actual output and decrease cyclical unemployment in the short run, but reduce its long-run rate of growth of potential output?

A   An increase in government spending on healthcare   ⬭

B   Net inward migration   ⬭

C   An increase in the national minimum wage   ⬭

D   An increase in the size of the government's budget deficit   ⬭

2 9 The diagram below shows the production possibility boundaries for an economy in year 1 (XX) and year 2 (YY).

Good A (vertical axis), Good B (horizontal axis)

What can be deduced from the diagram?

A Unemployment in year 2 was higher than in year 1

B The opportunity cost of producing good A remained constant in both years

C Direct taxes were higher in year 2 than in year 1

D The full capacity level of output was lower in year 2 than in year 1

3 0 A clothing manufacturer operating in an oligopolistic market structure prefers to use non-price competition rather than price competition when selling its clothing.

What could explain this behaviour?

A Advertising costs are too high for clothing in oligopolistic markets

B They expect the demand for their clothing to be price elastic with respect to a price fall

C They expect the demand for their clothing to be price inelastic with respect to a price fall

D It is difficult to generate brand loyalty when operating in an oligopoly

Answers to multiple choice questions

0 1 **C** – The marginal cost curve intersects the average cost curve at its minimum point. Therefore, when MC < AC the average cost curve will be downward sloping, hence average costs are falling. Similarly, for any level of output beyond MC = AC, average costs will be rising as MC > AC.

0 2 **C** – Restricting the power of trade unions provides greater labour market flexibility, improving productive capacity for the economy.

0 3 **D** – It is not the overall usefulness (total utility) that determines price (value), but the usefulness of each consecutive unit consumed (marginal utility). This can be explained by the 'diamond-water' paradox of value, where the value of an additional diamond is much greater than the value of an additional glass of water, despite water being far more useful, i.e. essential for survival. Since water is in such plentiful supply, the marginal utility of water is low, and as such, so is its price.

0 4 **B** – The marginal cost of labour is the additional cost of employing an extra worker. The number of workers has increased by one, and this has increased total labour cost (the wage bill) by $602.

0 5 **D** – When price elasticity of demand lies between 0 and –1, demand is price inelastic. A currency depreciation results in a fall in the price of exports. In response to the lower price, the quantity of exports demanded increases. However, if demand is price inelastic, the rise in quantity demanded is proportionately smaller than the fall in price resulting in a fall in export revenue.

0 6 **A** – Inferior goods are goods for which demand rises as income falls. This contrasts with normal goods for which demand falls when income falls. As instant noodles are classified as an inferior good, a fall in income will result in an increase in demand and an outward shift of the demand curve.

0 7 **C** – The Lorenz curve is a graphical representation of income distribution. It plots the cumulative percentage of income against the cumulative percentage of households.

0 8 **D** – Total revenue to the government is the tax per unit (the vertical distance between the two supply curves) multiplied by the number of units sold (0Q2).

0 9 **A** – A currency appreciation reduces the price of imports, easing cost pressures to firms as imported raw materials and component parts become cheaper for domestic producers. Therefore, with reduced production costs, SRAS shifts to the right.

1 0 **B** – Operating costs for companies are private costs, and have risen in this example. The cleaner production methods should reduce external costs, e.g. CO_2 emissions. Social costs = private costs + external costs, so the impact on social costs depends whether the rise in private costs is greater or less than the fall in external costs, and thus, is uncertain.

1 1 **C** – Quantitative easing increases the money supply for the economy which puts downward pressure on interest rates, and should have a stimulus effect on aggregate demand.

1 2 **D** – Trade between two countries, based on exploitation of comparative advantage, does not benefit either country if the rate of exchange does not lie between their opportunity cost ratios.

1 3 **C** – To calculate: (0.8 × 20%) + (0.2 × 40%) = 16% + 8% = 24%. Therefore, the index rises from 100 to 124.

1 4 **B** – At Q1, social costs are greater than private costs. Therefore, there are external costs and market failure has occurred. A lack of property rights is a common cause of market failure. Individuals and private firms are less likely to pollute property that they own.

1 5 C – AD is shown as falling, representing a decrease in economic growth and an increase in spare capacity. In the AD/AS model, LRAS is representative of the long-run trend rate of growth. Actual output Y2 (0.6%), is shown to have fallen below the long-run trend rate of Yfc (2.5%).

1 6 D – Because YED is positive, tea and coffee are considered substitute goods (they are in competitive demand). YED = % change in Qd/% change in P, i.e. 2.0 = % change in Qd/–10%. Rearranging the equation: % change in Qd = 2.0 × 10% = 20%

1 7 A – Curves DE and FG represent the short-run Phillips curve (SRPC). Changes in inflationary expectations can result in a shift of where the SRPC sits in relation to the origin.

1 8 D – One of the factors that can cause a shift in the supply of labour curve is an individual's preference. If there is an increased preference for leisure time, a worker will be less willing to work a given number of hours at any given wage rate.

1 9 B – The multiplier is calculated by 1/1–MPC, where MPC = marginal propensity to consume. The multiplier will therefore be 1/(1–0.8) = 1/0.2 = 5. This means the increase in national income will be five times the size of any injection into the economy (circular flow). So if investment is $6000m, national income will rise by $30,000m (5 × 6000).

2 0 A – Inflation increases the cost of living. Although the inflation rate fell, the price level is still rising, just at a slower rate.

2 1 C – Under a regressive tax system, there is an inverse relationship between the tax rate and the taxable income, i.e. the rate of taxation decreases as the income of taxpayers' increases.

2 2 D – Externalities are third-party effects arising from the production and consumption of goods and services where no appropriate compensation is paid, i.e. they are not included in the market price. These effects can be both positive and negative.

2 3 D – The Fisher equation is given by: MV = PT, where M = money supply, V = velocity of circulation, P = price level and T = output. If M increases by 6%, and P × T (the nominal value of national income) rises by 10%, then V must have increased.

2 4 A – In the short run, when there is only one variable factor of production, the law of diminishing returns states that the marginal cost of production (MC) will fall and then rise, as additional variable factors (workers) are combined with fixed factors (capital and land). The point at which MC is at its minimum will be when the marginal product of labour is at its maximum.

2 5 C – Both allocative and productive efficiency are required for economic efficiency to be achieved. Allocative efficiency can only be achieved when an economy is operating on the production possibility boundary, i.e. it is not possible to produce more of one good without producing less of another.

2 6 B – When output is at q1, MC > AC but below price. In the short run, the firm will increase output to q2, where MC = MR (profit maximisation). Firms operating in perfectly competitive markets have no influence on the market price.

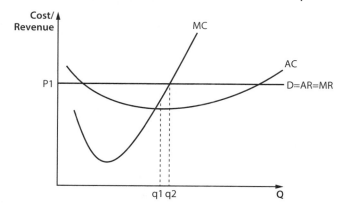

2 7 **C** – Real GNP per capita has already been adjusted for population size (per capita) and inflation (real). However, it does not reflect the value of the hidden or informal economy. Differences in the value of income earned from activity in the hidden economy, from one country to another, may reduce the reliability of national income measures such as GNP when comparing between countries.

2 8 **D** – An increase in government spending (increase the budget deficit) will provide a stimulus to aggregate demand and assist an economic recovery (upturn in the economic cycle), thus reducing cyclical unemployment. However, a rising budget deficit adds to national debt. As a result, future repayments may limit future growth potential, whilst all other options are likely to improve productive potential.

2 9 **D** – A production possibility curve shows the productive potential for an economy when all available resources are fully and efficiently employed, i.e. they represent the full potential level of output. An inward shift shows a fall in productive capacity.

3 0 **C** – Due to the interdependence of decision making, oligopolistic firms perceive their demand curve as being 'kinked' around the price level. They expect demand to be elastic with respect to a price rise and inelastic with respect to a price fall. This is based on the expected behaviour of competitors if they change their price. As a result, they expect revenue to fall, regardless of the price change, and will thus prefer non-price competition.

Paper 3 – Section B

Answer **ALL** questions in this section

Refer to the source material for extracts A, B, C and D

BREXIT: What's ahead for the UK?

INVESTIGATION

Scenario

You are an economist working for a government advisory group. You have been asked to report on the economic impact of the UK's decision to leave the European Union (so-called 'Brexit'). You have been asked to consider three key questions:

Question 3-1

How does trade between the UK and EU members compare with trade between the UK and non-EU countries, in terms of importance? Use the data in **Extract C** to support your assessment.

[10 Marks]

Question 3-2

Whilst some companies announced the possibility of moving operations out of the UK post-Brexit, many others affirmed their intention to remain, seemingly unconcerned about the possible effects.

Explain what companies, such as those in manufacturing, could do to remain competitive and prevent profits from falling despite the Brexit decision.

[15 Marks]

Question 3-3

Taking into account the news report, **Extract D**, and other evidence, evaluate the benefits of the UK's decision to exit the European Union.

[25 Marks]

Referring to the source documentation below, use **Extracts A, B and C** and your own economic knowledge to answer questions 3-1 and 3-2. There is also an additional news report, **Extract D**, which is to be used to help answer question 3-3.

Section B: Source Materials

Extract A: Impact of a UK exit from the EU

European Union (EU) member states are part of a customs union, with no tariffs on goods moving between them and a common tariff applied to goods entering from outside the EU. Member states cannot operate independent trade policies, for instance by pursuing bilateral free trade agreements with non-EU countries.

5 The central economic argument for/against membership of the EU is whether the benefits of membership of a large trading bloc exceed the drawbacks. Some argue that membership of the EU allows member states to benefit from better trade deals than they would be able to negotiate on their own.

It is often argued that being part of the EU makes a country a more attractive place to invest, as it
10 provides access via the single market to all member states. This can have benefits for the economy directly through the creation of jobs. The economy could also benefit indirectly from increased foreign direct investment (FDI) which may lead to improvements in productivity through the introduction of new working practices and transfers of technology that can also spread to local firms.

The UK is a major recipient of inward FDI and also an important investor in overseas economies.
15 The UK had the third highest stock of inward FDI in the world in 2014, behind the US and China.

Extract B: Brexit has multinationals warning of job cuts and lower profits.

Following the UK's referendum result, some of the world's largest companies warned they may relocate their British-based operations, placing thousands of jobs at risk. Facing concerns over the UK's ability to retain access to European markets, leaders in car manufacturing, aeronautics and banking were among those to announce reviews of their operations.

5 Amid the results' fallout were also announcements by companies related to profits. Sports Direct founder, Mike Ashley, warned that the collapse in the value of the Pound against the US Dollar could cause an increase in the cost of importing goods, lowering profits.

Warnings for workers in the City of London and its financial services sector, which employs more than 360,000 people, were of particular concern. These included the Chief Executive of JP Morgan, Jamie
10 Dimon, speculating that as many as 4,000 UK jobs might be moved abroad.

Potential job losses were also expected in industries other than financial services, with some of the country's largest manufacturers issuing warnings. Ford stated they will 'take whatever action is required' to ensure they remain competitive in the market. The vote for the UK to leave the EU was described as a 'lose-lose result for both Britain and Europe' by Tom Enders, the Chief Executive of
15 Airbus, which employs over 15,000 workers in the UK.

However, other manufacturers confirmed that they will maintain their UK operations and seem unlikely to make any significant changes in the near future. For example, Rolls-Royce and Jaguar Land Rover both set about to reassure workers that their jobs are safe. A spokesperson for Jaguar Land Rover said they 'remain committed to all their manufacturing sites and investment decisions'.

Extract C: UK Trade and FDI

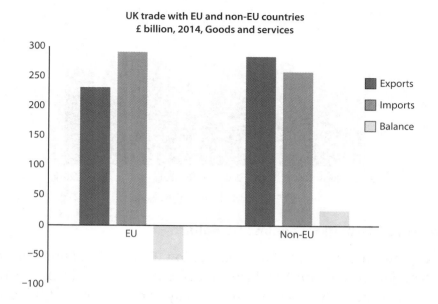

UK trade with EU and non-EU countries
£ billion, 2014, Goods and services

UK trade with EU and non-EU countries 2014
Goods and services

| | Exports | | Imports | | Balance |
	£ billion	%	£ billion	%	£ billion
EU	230	45%	289	53%	−59
Non-EU	283	55%	259	47%	+24
Total	513	100%	548	100%	−34

Source: ONS Balance of Payments Statistical Bulletin, Tables B & C

Top 10 UK export markets
Goods and services, 2014

		£ billion	% of total
1	US	88.0	17.1%
2	Germany	43.3	8.4%
3	Netherlands	34.1	6.6%
4	France	30.6	5.9%
5	Ireland	27.9	5.4%
6	Switzerland	22.9	4.4%
7	China	18.7	3.6%
8	Italy	16.3	3.2%
9	Belgium	15.6	3.0%
10	Spain	14.6	2.8%
	EU total	228.9	44.4%
	World total	515.2	100.0%

Source: ONS Pink Book, 2015, Table 9.3

Top 10 UK import markets
Goods and services, 2014

		£ billion	% of total
1	Germany	70.6	12.8%
2	US	51.6	9.4%
3	China	38.3	7.0%
4	France	37.0	6.7%
5	Netherlands	36.1	6.6%
6	Spain	26.1	4.7%
7	Belgium	24.1	4.4%
8	Italy	21.6	3.9%
9	Norway	21.0	3.8%
10	Ireland	17.1	3.1%
	EU total	290.6	52.9%
	World total	549.7	100.0%

Source: ONS Pink Book, 2015, Table 9.3

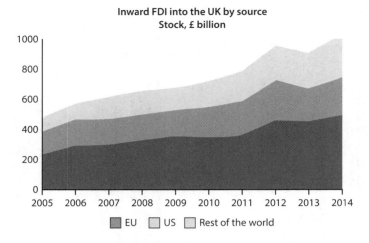

Inward FDI into the UK by source
Stock, £ billion

EU   US   Rest of the world

Extract D: Sterling reaches 31-year low against US dollar

The day after the UK's referendum on the European Union (EU), and the decision to exit, Sterling fell by 8% against the US dollar. In the months which followed its value fell by as much as 15% to reach $1.28, the lowest level in decades. At the time, many analysts predicted that it would fall even further. Uncertainty over the extent of an expected economic slowdown in the UK raised fears for investors
5 who began to look for safer destinations for their funds, selling Sterling assets.

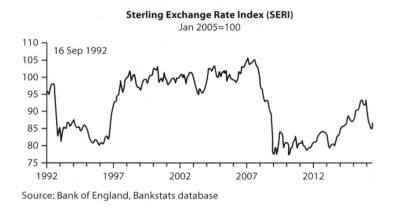

Sterling Exchange Rate Index (SERI)
Jan 2005=100

Source: Bank of England, Bankstats database

However, what may seem like a vulnerability could turn out not to be. At the time of the Brexit referendum, at 7% of GDP, the UK's current account deficit was at an all-time high. With a weak Pound exporters gain an edge in increasingly competitive global markets, the upside being a potential increase in export earnings, benefitting the economy as a whole. However, this view is seen
10 as weak by many as the rising cost of imported gadgets and foreign holidays, for example, is likely to outweigh any future gains made from trade.

Equally, although the value of Sterling fell significantly against the dollar, the story was not the same against other currencies. When looking at the 'trade-weighted' Sterling index, an indicator that is adjusted against a basket of currencies of the UK's main trading partners, although Sterling fell by 9%
15 after the referendum it remained 9.9% higher than previous lows in March 2009.

Mark scheme for Paper 3 – Section B

QUESTION 3-1

How does trade between the UK and EU members compare with trade between the UK and non-EU countries, in terms of importance? Use the data in **Extract C** to support your assessment.

[10 Marks]

Self-assessment

Self-assess your response using the grade descriptors and levels of response on pages 9 and 15–19.

Example response

Analyse the example response below. Consider how each of the grade descriptors is achieved using the annotations in the right hand column to help you. Go back and review your answer after analysing this response.

Possible response

Trade between the UK and EU members can be considered very important because the UK exports more to EU members than it does to any other country. Extract C shows 45% of the UK's total exports (230bn GBP) in 2014 goes to EU members. This large volume of trade provides a strong demand for exporting industries within the UK, stimulating economic growth and providing employment opportunities for UK workers. The revenue earned from this trade is also important for the UK's current account on balance of payments, which at the time was experiencing a large deficit.

> **AO2:** Explicit use of the data provided, including units (bn), year (2014) and, in this instance, currency (GBP).

> **AO1:** Shows good knowledge of the UK's current account position.

In comparison, trade between the UK and the US (a non-EU country) accounted for 17.1% of UK exports (88bn GBP) in 2014. Although not as large as the amount of trade with combined EU member states, this is still a significant figure and shows the US to be largest single nation export destination for the UK. This suggests important trade links exist between the UK and the US, without which additional pressure would be placed on the UK's existing current account deficit.

> **AO4:** This same point could also be made by saying that 'This (value of trade with the US) is more than twice the amount of exports to Germany, the largest single EU member nation receiving 8.4% of UK's exports (43.3b pounds) in 2014'.
>
> Good comparison between EU member nations and non-EU trading partner, the US.
>
> Explicit comment on 'importance' links the response to the question asked.

Extract C shows more trade is conducted in total with non-EU countries than with EU members. 55% of the UK's exports (283bn GBP) goes to non-EU countries. It is also significant to note that when considering the balance of trade, the UK has a surplus of 24bn GBP with non-EU countries whilst it has a trade deficit of 59bn GBP with the EU. This can be considered important for two reasons: ongoing trade with the EU contributes to the growing pressure on the current account deficit for the UK; imports from the EU play a large part in providing benefits of wider choice throughout the UK economy.

Trade with EU members is more important to the UK than trade with non-EU countries because the volume of trade conducted with the EU is so much larger than the nearest non-EU trading partner, the US. Without continued trade with the EU, the UK risks problems of reduced growth, rising unemployment, reduced efficiency and productivity, less innovation and less investment.

> **AO4:** A clear judgement is made, with justification based on the volume of trade, to answer the question asked.

Other areas for discussion:

- When comparing the top two countries trading with the UK, Germany and the US, the UK has a trade surplus of 36.4bn GBP with the US whilst it has a trade deficit of 27.3bn GBP with Germany.

- Imports to the UK from China are 38.3bn GBP (7% of total), and have been growing, whilst the UK only exports 18.7bn GBP (3.6% of total) to China.

- Although trade with the EU is obviously important to the UK, when looking at the contribution to overall trade of individual EU-member nations, the significance of any single member is less than that of non-EU trade partners such as the US. That said, there are only two non-EU nations, China and the US, in the top 10 trading partners with the UK, so as a group, EU-members are invaluable to the UK's trade.

- The UK is an open economy, actively engaged in extremely dynamic global markets and relies on trading with countries from all over the world. To make comparisons of the importance of trade with EU members and non-EU countries, based solely on the limited data presented in Extract C, will inevitably result in ill-informed judgements, and as such should be avoided.

- The UK's role in the global economy and its trade position with individual countries or groups of countries continues to change and evolve with time. Making static comparisons based on data from 2014 is misguided and limited, as this issue will require continual monitoring as time moves on.

- The importance of trade with the EU depends on the types of products that are being imported from the EU – capital goods, raw materials or finished consumer goods.

LevelUP: When making comparisons for this type of question you <u>MUST</u> make explicit use of the data provided. You can also draw on your own knowledge – here of UK trade with EU and non-EU members, for example – but make sure you respond to the data in the source material, and finish with a clear final judgement.

Self-reflection

Think about your overall response to this question and note down at least one:

- **what went well** (WWW) – something you did well in your response
- **even better if** (EBI) – something you could have done better

Keep these points in mind and use them to improve your next attempt at an essay question.

QUESTION 3-2

Whilst some companies announced the possibility of moving operations out of the UK post-Brexit, many others affirmed their intention to remain, seemingly unconcerned about the possible effects.

Explain what companies, such as those in manufacturing, could do to remain competitive and prevent profits from falling despite the effects of the Brexit decision.

[15 Marks]

Self-assessment

Self-assess your response using the grade descriptors and levels of response on pages 9 and 15–19.

Example response

As a result of the Brexit decision, UK firms may lose access to some EU markets as a result of trade barriers imposed on their exports to EU member countries. They may also experience rising import costs from a weaker pound (extract B), making imported raw materials, components parts and finished goods more expensive. This reduces their competitiveness in international markets and lowers profits. This can be shown as increasing costs from AC1-AC2 in fig. 1, resulting in a fall in profit: P1bcd → P2efg as shown.

AO1: Shows understanding of the impact of rising costs on competitiveness and profit.

AO2: Applies extract information about falling currency value to the context of manufacturing.

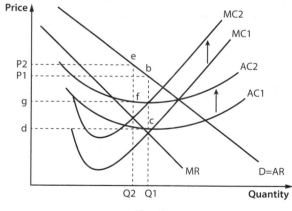

Fig. 1

To remain competitive when facing rising costs firms may need to invest in improved technology; using more capital intensive methods of production. In industries such as manufacturing, a more automated approach improves labour productivity by reducing the number or workers needed. It should also raise

AO1: Shows knowledge and understanding of improved technology to remain competitive.

AO2: Applies technological improvements to manufacturing industries (i.e. to the context of the question).

the speed of production and increase output. In addition, more mechanised production methods are also likely to improve the quality of goods produced and reduce costs resulting from wastage due to defects and human error. This may, in the longer term, result in higher profits than previously earned.

> **AO3:** Develops logical chain of reasoning and links back to the question with comment on higher profits.

However, many producers manufacture goods that require more labour intensive methods, e.g. jewellery, that cannot be easily automated. These firms can improve the training of their workers to increase their skill and productivity. Improving the skills of workers through improved training not only raises productivity, but will also improve the quality of the work done by those employed. Better quality jewellery would allow firms to raise their prices and may also increase demand for their goods, i.e. an outward shift of AR = D, helping to prevent reduced profits from higher material costs.

> **AO2:** Gives a specific example (jewellery making) of a labour intensive industry.
>
> **AO1:** Shows knowledge and understanding of training and its effect on labour productivity.
>
> **AO3:** Uses logical chain of reasoning to explain how improving labour skills can help prevent falling profits.

A significant cost to many manufacturers is their human capital. Car manufacturers, for example, could look to lower costs by reducing the working hours of some staff to improve their competitiveness. They may even go so far as to reduce the number of workers, making redundancies, further lowering their marginal costs. Alternatively, they may be able to reduce labour costs by lowering their wages to certain members of their workforce. In fact, some combination of these three methods is likely to be used to try and prevent profits falling.

A longer-term approach to remaining competitive is investing more into research and development of new products and improving designs. For companies such as Airbus, operating in the aeronautics industry, quality of design and producing the very best, most advanced equipment is imperative. Rising costs and subsequent price rises to prevent reduced profits are more likely to be accepted by customers if they are guaranteed to be purchasing the best the market has to offer. Without continued, or perhaps increased investment into research and development, firms such as Airbus may struggle to remain competitive.

> **AO2:** Good application making explicit use of extract material.

> **AO2/AO3:** Good development of logical chain of reasoning, related to Airbus and the aeronautics industry.

Other areas for discussion:

- Increased productivity could result in lower costs, which may enable a firm to lower prices to increase sales

- Source cheaper materials and suppliers

- Switch to domestic suppliers

- Advertise to increase sales and revenue

- Improve customer relations and service (before and after sales)

- Offshore part of their operations, e.g. call centres or manufacturing base to gain access to cheaper labour

- Relocate their factories closer to the source of raw materials to reduce transportation costs

- Seek out new export markets abroad, e.g. via the internet

- Diversify their range of products
- Do nothing – let the depreciation of the Sterling make their exports more competitive abroad, thereby increasing export sales with non-EU trading partners

LevelUP: The question asks you to explain what companies 'such as' those in manufacturing could do to remain competitive and prevent profits from falling. To score marks for **application** you should try to give manufacturing examples – and, better still, use those in the source material; Airbus and Jaguar Land Rover, for example. However, the 'such as' phrase does give you a 'get-out-of-jail' card. If you really can't think of any manufacturing examples you could use others. If you can, stick to manufacturing, but if you are (really, really) stuck use a phrase like 'Other than manufacturing, firms such as those in the service industry...' to signal to the examiner the change in focus.

Self-reflection

Think about your overall response to this question and note down at least one:

- **what went well** (WWW) – something you did well in your response
- **even better if** (EBI) – something you could have done better

Keep these points in mind and use them to improve your next attempt at an essay question.

QUESTION 3-3

Taking into account the news report, **Extract D**, and other evidence, evaluate the benefits of the UK's referendum decision to exit the European Union.

[25 Marks]

Self-assessment

Self-assess your response using the grade descriptors and levels of response on pages 9 and 15–19.

Example response

The European Union (EU) is a customs union; a form of economic integration where there are no trade barriers between member nations and a common external tariff imposed on all non-members. EU nations are also part of a single market that allows

AO1: Shows understanding of a customs union and single market.

free movement of people and resources (both physical and financial) between all member states.

After exiting the EU, the UK may benefit from the ability to negotiate better trade deals and reduce its reliance on a potentially weakening EU economy. That said, the UK may also face threats of rising costs to UK firms when trading with EU members, increased inflationary pressure from a weakened currency and the potential for reduced foreign direct investment (FDI) inflows.

AO1: Paragraph identifies possible effects of the UK exiting the EU.

As a non-EU member, the UK would be free to negotiate bilateral free trade agreements with other non-EU countries (extract A), including its largest single trade partner, the US. As a result of this, the US export market for the UK is likely to grow as US consumers and firms would have access to more competitively priced UK-produced goods and services. This would lead to increased employment opportunities for workers in the UK's export industries. UK firms looking to establish themselves in global markets would also benefit from increased access to the US market, particularly small and medium-sized enterprises. The potential for export growth to the US is particularly important to the UK as it held a trade deficit with the US of 8.3b GBP (extract C) in 2014. Furthermore, increased export to the US may lead to an increase in aggregate demand and an improvement in the UK's economic growth.

AO2: Good use of extract and application to the US.

AO4: Judgement made regarding the importance of trade to UK with the US.

AO2: Good use of data from extract to support judgement about importance.

There may also be benefits for UK consumers. As shown in fig. 1 below, UK consumers may benefit from welfare gains (area P2abP1) resulting from reduced tariffs on US imports into the UK, which lowers the price from P2 → P1.

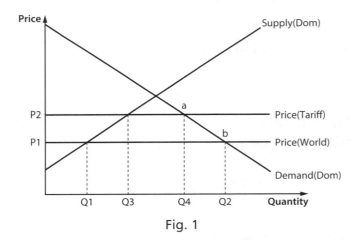

Fig. 1

However, these benefits may be offset to some extent by the imposition of tariffs on exports to EU countries. This is likely to reduce the price competitiveness of UK firms in Europe, with the imposition of the common external tariff on UK goods and services making them relatively more expensive to EU consumers and firms. Of particular importance is the potential effect this may have on firms operating in the financial sector, a leading source of export earnings and FDI, with some large investment banks already considering moving their operations out of the UK (extract B). These concerns may prove to be unwarranted, but the early warning signs are that the UK's position as a global leader in financial services may weaken in the near future should access to EU markets diminish.

AO4/AO2: Uses the importance of the financial sector to the UK economy, linked to information from the extract (AO2), to comment on significance of likely effects from Brexit.

Exiting the EU may also make the UK a less appealing place for foreign firms to set up, leading to a reduction in FDI inflows into the UK. The UK is currently one of the world's top FDI destinations, which benefits the economy directly through increased employment opportunities, and indirectly through improved training opportunities and working practices, higher productivity and access to the latest technologies (extract A). The UK's attractiveness as an FDI destination, though, is determined by a range of factors and not EU membership alone. The UK has sound future growth opportunities and a good track record of fiscal stability when compared to many other economies. It has a growing number of software development programmes, for instance, and continues to be a European leader in research and development. This makes a significant fall in FDI as a result of exiting the EU less likely.

AO3/AO2: Provides explanation, linked to the extract material (AO2), of the potential negative effect of reduced FDI inflows.

AO4/AO2: Paragraph applies knowledge and understanding of the UK economy to provide good critical reasoning as to why the expected fall in FDI is unlikely following Brexit.

Since the referendum result, the value of Sterling has fallen dramatically (Extract D). A weakened currency adds cost-push inflationary pressure to the UK as the price of imports increases for UK firms and consumers. As such, many households may experience an increase in the cost of living, e.g. more expensive mobile phones and foreign holidays, reducing living standards. Firms reliant on imported raw materials or imported finished goods are likely to see a reduction in profits. As a result they may increase prices, putting further pressure on inflation.

AO2: Draws on information provided in the extract.

AO3: Provides reasoning for expected negative effect on UK households and firms of a weakened currency.

However, for exporters looking to establish new trade deals, a weaker currency provides a competitive advantage (Extract D) as their goods and services will become relatively cheaper in global markets. Although valid in theory, the beneficial impact of a weaker currency to the UK is questionable. Considering the UK's large and growing surplus on trade in services, non-price factors are of more significance to export performance. A depreciation of the exchange rate would be more important for economies specialising in cheaper manufactured goods, such as China, where price competitiveness is a key determinant.

AO1/AO2: Uses the extract material to identify benefit of currency depreciation.

AO4: Offers evaluation of the theoretical effect of currency depreciation when applied to the UK's context.

To conclude, at the time the source material was written, new free trade agreements were yet to be negotiated and the specifics of the UK's future relationship with the EU was undecided. Potential drops in FDI may be offset by focusing on continued improvement of productivity and competitiveness. Although some inflationary effects may be experienced from a weakened currency, the pound may yet recover from its initial decline. Based on the information provided, it is not possible to say whether the potential benefits to the UK outweigh the risks of exiting the EU.

AO4: A good, clear conclusion drawn, identifying why there is too much uncertainty to make any definitive judgments on the issue.

In your own answer you could use more recent knowledge. How has the referendum decision played out over time? Use your understanding to comment on the current situation, comparing and contrasting that to the source material.

Other areas for discussion:

- Better control over immigration. However, this reduces the ability of UK labour to access EU employment markets and there is no guarantee that immigration will be reduced; depends on immigration policy, plus political and moral pressure.

- Wages may rise, particularly for low skilled workers, as the supply of cheap labour from the EU is reduced.

- Public funds previously devoted to EU membership now available for domestic investment and/or paying down debt. However, fiscal dividends may be offset by loss of trade and reduced growth.

- Rising cost pressure to UK firms may lead to innovation and productivity gains. However, these may not be possible in some competitive industries, or may not be enough.

- Reduced regulatory controls, (e.g. CAP) allowing more freedom to domestic producers.

- Trade creation and trade diversion effects of non-EU membership.

- A unilateral free trade approach by the UK helps to lower prices and reduce administrative costs of implementing selective protectionist policies. However, may be difficult to maintain if other nations impose import tariffs on UK goods and services.

- Greater independence for UK government policy unbridled from EU controls. However, there is no guarantee of improvement. This is largely dependent on the effectiveness of UK government.

LevelUP: The difference between a Level 4 (very good) and a Level 5 (excellent) response is the amount of critical evaluation. Generic evaluation such as 'long-run/short-run comparison', 'costs versus benefits' and 'other factors to consider' etc, are not enough for top marks – your evaluation needs to be specific, detailed and critical. In particular, it needs to be contextual and apply directly to the case studies and the question at hand.

Self-reflection

Think about your overall response to this question and note down at least one:

- **what went well** (WWW) – something you did well in your response

- **even better if** (EBI) – something you could have done better.